Praise for *Nine Secrets for Getting Elected*

"Whether you are a first-time candidate or a veteran of a dozen races, whether you have to raise $1,000, $100,000, a million, or are self-funding, whether your opponents are homecoming kings and queens or rogues a "half a bubble off of level," Kit Bobko has written the indispensable introduction to actually winning elections. *Nine Secrets for Getting Elected* is a wonderful, funny, and—amazingly—detailed and useful guide to how to actually win the next round at the polls. Tens of thousands of candidates every single year pull their papers without a clue about what to do next (or what they ought to have done first) but Bobko lays it all out, A to Z, with a delightful narrative of local elected life that transcends any city's boundaries and even the state and federal levels to provide a winning—and very funny—guide to the great unknown land of electioneering.

You don't need to hire a high-priced professional to win the seat you have been longing to fill—at least not right away—but you do need to read this book. *Nine Secrets for Getting Elected* has the scoop you need right now to win that race next cycle."

—HUGH HEWITT, lawyer, law professor, multi-Emmy award-winning broadcast journalist, and *NYT* bestselling author

"*Nine Secrets for Getting Elected* will help you do just that! It's a smart and fascinating take from a guy who's been where the rubber meets the road, deep inside the kind of politics that really determine our quality-of-life. It's the good, the bad, and the funny. But if you're serious about real politics read *Nine Secrets for Getting Elected!*"

—KURT SCHLICHTER, Senior Columnist for Townhall.com, lawyer, retired Army Infantry colonel, former stand-up comic

Nine Secrets for Getting Elected

Nine Secrets for Getting Elected

The Official Manual for Candidates
from City Hall to the Statehouse and Beyond

Kit Bobko
Former two-term Mayor and
City Councilman of Hermosa Beach

Copyright © 2017 by Kit Bobko

All rights reserved. No part of this book may be used or reproduced in any manner whatsoever without prior written consent of the publisher except in the case of brief quotations embodied in critical articles and reviews. Special book excerpts or customized printings can be created to fit specific needs.

ISBN:

Book design by Dotti Albertine

Printed in the United States of America

Don't bounce it; they'll boo you.

—Derek Jeter to George W. Bush before he threw out the first pitch at Game 3 of the 2001 World Series

---

Now, I think we should aim in our public discourse for debate that is rational, that is civil, and that is conducted in the spirit of goodwill. But important ideas are sometimes disturbing. They may offend. Self-government is not for the faint of heart.

—US Supreme Court Justice Samuel Alito
Newport Beach, California, February 11, 2017

CONTENTS

Introduction	*xiii*
Secret No. 1 – Know Why You Are Running	**1**
Preparing for the Campaign	4
Dirty Politics	11
Losing Is Inevitable, but It Isn't the End	17
Look Out for Scandals	18
Keeping the Press Close	21
Minding the Fallout	27
Secret No. 2 – Get Comfortable Asking for Money	**31**
Asking for Money	31
Spending Your Money Wisely	36
What's in a Name?	39
Negative Advertising	43
The People in Your Corner Matter	46
Back to the Gallery . . .	54
Secret No. 3 – Know Thyself	**60**
What's a Nice Candidate Like You Doing in a Place Like This?	60
Where Do You Come From?	63

Contents

Where Are You Going?	64
Where Are You Vulnerable?	66
Will You Endorse Me?	68
Making Enemies	73
Sheep's Clothing	78
Taking Your District's Temperature	82
Keep Your Nose Out of My Rice Bowl	88

Secret No. 4 – Pick Your Battles   **94**
Politics Is a Contact Sport	94
Know Your Opponents	102
The Same Old Song	105
Where It All Went Wrong	110

Secret No. 5 – Be Prepared for the Ridiculousness   **118**
Canaries in the Political Coal Mine	118
Example 1: Dr. D	118
Example 2: Beecher	119
Example 3: Anti-Oil Evangelica	120
Dreams and Ambition	120
Wort? That Just Sounds Bad	121
The Quest for Approval	125
Politically Expedient Hidey-Holes	127
The Final Showdown	129
Some People Don't Like the Smell of Grape-Nuts	139

Secret No. 6 – Be Principled (Even When It Hurts)   **142**
It All Started So Well . . .	142
. . . And Then Things Went South	145

Contents

Oily Roots	149
Leadership Matters	150
Management Is Not Leadership	155
The Arrow Missed the Apple	161
"A Full-Scale Internal Affairs Arachnicide Investigation"	164
Political Pornography	171

Secret No. 7 – Know What You Don't Know — 175

How Much Do You Know About Your Trash?	176
The Big E	180
When You Don't Know What You Need to Know	185
Hollow Symbolism	188

Secret No. 8 – Have a Motor — 193

What's Past Is Prologue	193
We Don't Have to Make Peace with Our Friends	200
Politics Is the Art of the Possible	207
Can You Afford to Serve?	212
When Bankruptcy Isn't an Option	212
Fiscal Rocks and Political Hard Places	217

Secret No. 9 – Know Some People Won't Like You — 223

Have a Good Story to Tell	223
A Phone Call Changed Everything	227
Black or Green?	236

Conclusion	*253*
How Can We Help You Win?	*257*

INTRODUCTION

Can you do it? the Little League president asked me.

Of course, I answered, thinking he'd assumed I might be otherwise occupied on that particular Saturday morning, so busy that I wouldn't have time to throw out the ceremonial first pitch of the Hermosa Beach Little League season.

Good, he said. *You played baseball, right?*

That's when it struck me that he wasn't inquiring about my availability to throw the baseball, but my *ability* to throw a baseball.

No. Never did. But I can throw a baseball.

Of course I could. I was a red-blooded American. The first sports poster in my room as a kid was of (then) phenom pitcher Doc Gooden in full stretch. I remember watching in awe as Kirk Gibson hobbled around the bases after a walk-off home run in the 1988 World Series. Like everyone outside of New York, I reflexively rooted against the Yankees.

Okay, good. A measurable amount of doubt had seeped into his voice. I guess everyone who tried to deliver the pitch said the same thing.

Just try to aim high, he said. *Whatever you do, don't bounce it in.*

Introduction

The distance from the mound to home plate was what, forty feet in Little League? I could do that left-handed. No problem.

～

Of all the things I learned in politics, the advice the Little League President gave me that day was probably the best—*don't bounce it in*. There are any number of ways to miss the strike zone in baseball and in politics. I could throw over the catcher's head, or too far to the right or to the left. But the only unforgivable sin was leaving the pitch short. Not giving it enough zip.

Everyone wants to see their leaders square up and fire it in.

When Opening Day came, I resolved to summon my inner Roger Clemens and fire a heater right down the middle of the plate. And by *heater*, I mean the best 51 mph fastball I could muster.

On Opening Day, all the Little Leaguers in Hermosa Beach gather for individual introductions, followed by a ceremonial lap with their team. Parents cheer from just outside the baseline as a rainbow of too-big uniforms animated by precocious six- to thirteen-year-olds circle the bases. I walked around talking to the parents during the ceremony.

After the initial greeting, the conversation with the assembled dads always turned to the first pitch.

You ready?

Sure, I said. And I laughed. *I think I can handle it.*

Good, you'll be fine. Just don't bounce it in.

Thanks for the tip. I would laugh and venture somewhere else in the crowd and talk to someone else I knew. And I would have the same conversation.

Introduction

You got this?
Yeah. No problem.
Cool. Just don't bounce it in.

By the fourth conversation I started wondering—is there something more to this than I understand? It's just throwing a baseball forty feet. I've been throwing baseballs, basketballs, footballs, water polo balls, horseshoes, and everything else an American male could throw for my entire life. What is everyone so worried about?

I found a friend whose twelve-year-old son, Jack, was a player. He gave me one of his team's caps to wear during the ceremony.

Mind if I borrow Jack for a few minutes? I want to warm up before the big pitch.

Why, you getting worried? my friend asked, chuckling.

Of course not. I just needed to warm up the ol' arm.

Good idea. Get loose. The last thing you want to do is bounce it in.

No, the last thing I wanted to do was have another person tell me not to bounce it in. Nobody tells the guy standing on the free throw line *Don't miss.* Nobody tells the fullback about to get the ball *Don't fumble.* But every Little League dad I spoke to that morning was doing exactly that.

When Jack and I finished, I asked him if he would catch the first pitch for me. He was excited to do it. I'd also seen during the time we were warming up that he was an exceptional little athlete, and his athleticism would probably be able to cover up any miscues on my part.

When the ceremonial part of Opening Day ended, the president of the Little League lined the kids on either side of the pitcher's mound along the first and third base lines. Their dads, wearing the same caps as their sons and daughters, stood behind them. There were probably three hundred eyes watching to see if I was going to make it across the plate.

I gave Jack a nod and he jogged to his spot. The Little League president made an announcement that the mayor was going to throw the first pitch, and with as much fanfare as the Hermosa Beach Little League could muster, he handed me the ceremonial ball.

Jack, now in position, crouched down and gave his pitcher a target. I leaned forward, the baseball resting on the small of my back, and suddenly realized this might be more difficult than I'd thought.

Jack, a slight twelve-year-old boy in a catcher's crouch, presented a target no bigger than a laundry basket. Worse yet, he had a twelve-year-old's hand inside a twelve-year-old's mitt. Fully extended, Jack's glove was the size of a salad plate. Or maybe a cantaloupe. If hitting this target at this distance were a game at the county fair, nobody would play.

Don't bounce it in ringing in my ears, I remembered that Jack was a good little ballplayer, and he probably had buddies who threw as hard as I did. He was going to catch it. I just needed to get it close.

I stood up, reached back, and threw my best semblance of a heater at the twelve-year-old catcher crouched forty feet away.

Nice throw! the president said, visibly pleased the mayor of his town hadn't tried to patty-cake it in. *We've seen all kinds over*

Introduction

the years, he said. To everyone's great relief, but mostly mine, I hadn't bounced it in.

It was okay to miss. People expected that sometimes. Madison Bumgarner didn't always throw strikes. Clayton Kershaw didn't have a perfect game every time he took the mound.

With a crowd watching and expectations mounting, it was easy to see why some people had trouble throwing a decent pitch. But the key for the first pitch, as in politics, was to keep your eye on the target, disregard the chatter, reach back, and do your best to zip it across the plate.

⁓

This book is the culmination of my time in elected office in the sun-splashed seaside city of Hermosa Beach, California. Hermosa Beach is a quirky, independent, newly wealthy and completely unpredictable 1.4-square-mile city, blessed with beautiful beaches and a short memory. During the day, volleyballers play on the postcard-white beaches, and at night college students and young people pack into the city's bars and restaurants. Hermosa Beach boasts a world-famous jazz club (the Lighthouse—maybe you saw it in *La La Land*), and a Walk of Fame for pioneering surfers; these attractions are located within one hundred feet of each other. Professional athletes and Olympians call my city home. Palatial mansions stand next to termite-eaten beach bungalows. And that's fine. What everybody who lives here loves best about Hermosa Beach is that nobody gives much of a damn about what anyone else is doing. And everyone likes it that way.

Introduction

My first city manager told me that when he arrived in Hermosa Beach in the 1980s, it was common for him to see one old couch sitting on the curb in the morning on trash day, and a different one on the same curb when he passed at lunch. *Someone had decided to upgrade*, he said. By the time I was elected to city council in 2006, much had changed.

But not that much.

Many of the stories in this book reflect the uniqueness of Hermosa Beach. There isn't any place on Earth that can boast a cast of elected officials like the ones we've elected. Our former treasurer, David Cohn, would give disgraced former congressman Anthony Weiner and his famous south-of-the-equator selfies a run for their money. As you will soon learn, in affairs of the heart—as in politics—some things are best left to the imagination.

On the other hand, many of the situations reflected in the pages that follow are common to every city in California. The challenges presented by the public employee unions, unfunded pension liabilities, and seedy politicians are not unique to my city. The difficulty of starting a business, large or small, is unfortunately not a problem peculiar to Hermosa, and events in my city are a microcosm of larger statewide issues. As you will see, this is especially true for start-ups, and doubly true in Hermosa Beach if the start-up wants to brew beer.

Other examples in this book exemplify problems that exist both in California and throughout the nation. As Wallace Stegner once wrote, "California is like the rest of the United States—only more so." The debate Hermosa Beach had over the right to drill for oil is the same debate that states in the

Introduction

Midwest are having over the XL Pipeline, the same debate that towns in Pennsylvania are having over fracking. The Anti-Oil Evangelicals you will read about in this book exist anywhere that sees a debate about oil. The only things separating the debates over Big-E environmentalism that occurred in the Hermosa Beach city council chambers from the ones that occur on the floor of the House of Representatives are the stakes.

And the politics. The difference between local and national politics is only a matter of degree. The public employee unions' shenanigans are not confined to my city, or to California. My battles with the Hermosa Beach police union were just a local skirmish in a broader philosophical war between public employee unions' unquenchable demand for *more* and people who understand that there is simply no more to give. Governor Scott Walker fought the same battles with his public unions in Wisconsin. Rahm Emanuel has done the same in Chicago, just as former mayor Chuck Reed has in San Jose. Incidentally, Reed and Emanuel are both Democrats, which proves that the fights with the public employee unions are no more ideological than any other dispute over money. Other political fisticuffs are just about power. The deals and the backroom wrangling happen everywhere. The dirty tricks do too.

But mostly, this book is a chance to pull back the stage curtain and see how the political rabbits are smuggled into the government hat. It's a chance to see how the government—your government—works. The stories in this book are about the vast majority of good, dedicated people who are truly in the public's service, and the handful of really bad ones who claim to be. Hopefully, this book will shine a light on how we currently govern ourselves, and hopefully it will inform voters so they can demand that the people they trust to govern do it better. And if they fail, I hope you'll take the lessons of this book to heart and run for office yourself.

This book represents the ups and downs of seven and a half years in local government in Hermosa Beach, California. Everything you are about to read actually happened. Only the names have been changed.

SECRET No. 1
Know Why You Are Running

Nobody runs for public office just for the hell of it.

Campaigning is hard, even if you're a naturally outgoing and charismatic person, and being in public office is often stressful, sometimes contentious, and can be emotionally draining. Serving on a local board or city council certainly isn't lucrative, and it inevitably takes time away from work, friends, and family.

So why do it?

Well, say you're a decent, rational, public-spirited citizen. You've got just as much of an eye for injustice as I do, and there's probably something about your city (or county/state/country) that you *know* could be fixed. Or something that could be done better or less expensively if *They* just pulled *Their* heads out of the sand for a second and looked around. It's not brain surgery, after all . . . or is it?

That frustration is often the first step toward a run for public office, and it's the easiest. Anyone who interacts with the government has felt it.

The good news is that you're not alone.

Clint Eastwood once felt the same way. And the thing that finally spurred him to run for public office was ice cream.

In 1986, the *Dirty Harry* actor wanted to erect a small building in downtown Carmel, California—a sleepy city in picturesque Monterey County nestled along the Pacific Coast—but the town council rejected his plans. Feeling unfairly hassled by the city's innumerable rules, regulations, taxes, zoning laws, building permit requirements, and endless red tape, Eastwood decided he'd had enough and resolved to take on city hall. He ran for mayor on a platform of reforming Carmel's ridiculously stringent and outdated rules for development and zoning—one of which prohibited the sale of ice cream cones.

You're probably not Clint Eastwood, but you should know that even he had to fight stereotypes and convince voters he was serious. He had to stop being an actor and campaign. That's the hurdle that every candidate has to clear. And as is true for many competitive endeavors, the rules of the game are the same for all participants. But some players are better than others.

First things first: In this great nation, anyone can run for office. We used to say any kid can grow up to be president, and that's still true. You don't have to be a professional politician. You don't have to have a PoliSci degree or years of experience working in the public sector. You *do* need to know what you want to use the office for, however, and your reasoning should be strong enough to sustain a full campaign. The truth is that all it takes to spark a run for office is the will to take on city hall. Maybe the spark comes from something as mundane as a rule against selling ice cream cones. Maybe it comes from something else. The spark comes first. Everything else comes after.

You've already got the will, don't you? You already know what you want to fix. You know why you want to serve. The spark is there.

This book is about all the things that come next.

Secret No. 1 – Know Why You Are Running

∽

Phone calls from certain people at certain times mean only one thing—something bad has happened. As a politician, this is particularly true when a reporter calls unexpectedly in the middle of the afternoon on a random weekday.

On this November afternoon, the beat reporter for our local daily newspaper was on the other end of the line. The reporter was a talented young guy, probably in his late twenties. He was relatively new to covering Hermosa Beach, but had shown a genuine interest in getting the facts right. I appreciated his diligence and wanted to help him get the story straight. Let's call him Jimmy Olsen.

Hey Kit, Jimmy Olsen from the Daily Breeze. Olsen always gave me the full-name introduction with each phone call, even though he was the only reporter I spoke with regularly at that paper. *Got a minute?* I could hear the anxiety and excitement in his voice.

Sure, what's up? Olsen was a good barometer of which stories actually had legs, so I never passed on a chance to chat and find out what he knew.

You hear anything about the treasurer and an extortion plot?

∽

David Cohn (actual name) was the city's recently elected seventy-two-year-old treasurer. If you squinted and the lighting was bad, Cohn might remind you of a paler version of Danny DeVito, minus whatever it is that makes Danny DeVito likable.

The residents of Hermosa Beach had elected him to office in November 2011, ousting longtime resident and eighteen-year city treasurer John Workman (actual name).

Workman was quintessential Old Hermosa and couldn't have been more different from the man who replaced him. A big, quietly jovial, mustachioed man with a wry sense of humor, Workman had the plainspoken manner you would expect from someone born in a place called Red Oak, Iowa. He had lived in Hermosa Beach since 1968 and was the longtime owner of the neighborhood TriAngle Hardware store. Workman had been the Chamber of Commerce's Man of the Year in 1989, and he still volunteered for the Rotarians and delivered Meals on Wheels for the Salvation Army. When I first met him, I'd immediately recognized he was one of the good guys.

Unlike Cohn, Workman didn't have a finance degree or his Series 7 certification; he was a successful small businessman who managed a portfolio of rental properties all over Southern California. In a small city like ours, Workman's practical experience and common sense were more than enough qualification for public office.

More important, John Workman's decency was palpable, and for the better part of two decades, the people of Hermosa Beach kept him in office because they felt they could trust him with their money.

Preparing for the Campaign

Campaign specifics will vary according to the district, the office being sought, and the candidate, but there are a few constants.

First, be sure that you're qualified to run. Not everyone is (no one under thirty-five can be POTUS, for instance), and you don't want to mistakenly mount an expensive, time-consuming campaign for an office you won't be permitted to occupy. Before you do anything else, check the list of qualifications with your local city clerk or the county registrar.

Second, you're going to want to find a campaign manager. This person doesn't have to be a professional, but he or she should be organized, energetic, and willing to do the work of helping you draft a political plan, a budget, and a timeline, which should start the day you decide to run and end on election day. The timeline should include all the pertinent filing deadlines, financial reporting deadlines, voter registration dates, and the date that absentee ballots are projected to go out. The timeline should also include important community dates, like city council and chamber of commerce meetings. The timeline can also incorporate your own deadlines, like monthly fundraising goals and outreach events.

From fundraising to sit-down coffees with voters, there's a lot to do, and not a lot of time to do it in, which is why an action-plan/timeline is necessary. Start with the legal deadlines and fit the rest in around them. Check the website for the office you're campaigning for; the relevant legal deadlines should be found in the "Election Calendar" section. Make sure you understand what you'll need to do to meet these deadlines. Filing to run for office might just mean filling out a form, but it might also require a filing fee or signatures from voters in your district. For example, in Hermosa Beach, a candidate has to collect signatures of thirty registered voters in the district. If you leave this to the last minute, and for whatever reason only collect the signatures of twenty-nine registered voters, guess what? Your name won't appear on the ballot. Similarly, for financial reporting deadlines, you'll need to know how often you're required to report the money you've raised, or face a fine.

Once you have a timeline, dive deeper into the process and create a political plan of action. This plan should help you refine your fundraising goals, which will make your timeline even clearer. Your political plan of action should look something like this:

- Write up an overview of the office you're running for. Research past elections for that seat and try to work out how much of the vote you'll need to win.

- Research past candidates' financial reports. Pay particular attention to their income and expenditures.

- Work out specific targets for your mailers. Determine whether different voter demographics need to be presented with different messages.

- Start working on an updated biography that highlights your community involvement and particular qualifications for office. Start early on this; it's harder than you think.

- Make a list of the community organizations you must meet with. Target groups that already have established lists of members, because they can help with e-mail. Make time in your schedule to go to their meetings and introduce yourself.

- Build a grassroots plan for which homes need to be walked and which need to be called. "Walking wins" is a cliché in local politics, but there isn't any substitute for walking precincts, knocking on doors, and talking to voters one on one. This is especially true for the high-propensity voters. It's best to call homes with low-propensity voters so they can talk to you or a volunteer about your campaign. These voters need first to be persuaded to vote, and then to be persuaded to vote for you. High-propensity voters, who will vote no matter what, need only be convinced that you are the one to vote for.

- Have a plan for how to use people who volunteer to help you. If someone wants to spend a few hours working on the campaign, make sure you have something for them to do!

Once you've got an action plan worked out, the nitty-gritty of marketing yourself should be your next priority. Have professional photographs of yourself taken. These photos should capture your essence, your connection to the community. Think landmarks or popular community improvement projects. Photos can mean a thousand things, so make your photos meaningful. Remember, your campaign photo may be the only time many voters ever see you. A good photo will leave a good impression with voters; a bad one can kill you. Don't scrimp on your campaign photo.

Next, take the time to write out your message clearly—this isn't the time for ambiguity or slogans—and tailor it to the needs of your community. At the time of my first campaign, Hermosa Beach had seen a recent uptick in development that worried a good number of people. They felt that the town was growing too quickly without the input of its citizens—that they were losing control of their town. My campaign was able to respond to that concern and build our message around it: "Let's keep Hermosa Beach a place that changes people. Let's not let people change Hermosa Beach."

Every election has an issue that resonates with people. The key is to tie your message, your slogan, and yourself to that issue, and keep tightening that knot.

To figure out which issue you want to use, do a little detective work by building a base in the community. Whether it's your church, sports teams, or schools, there's always a way to involve yourself in your community's beating heart, and it's there that you'll meet the fifty or so people who can inform you and influence what the community cares about. Every town has its own group of movers and shakers, and you will not get your message across without winning over these community bellwethers. Be careful—there isn't a list of these people on any website. You'll only learn who they are by showing up to a community project and getting involved.

Your message needs to be a clearly defined description of what you want to accomplish in office, and it needs to appear on your website, on social media, and in your mailers. Once you've defined your message, you can work on your slogan. Your slogan should be a distilled version of your overall message, a quick sound bite you can attach to your name to tell the voter who you are and what your message is. Plaster that slogan on your website, your campaign literature, your buttons, your hats—everything. Do not let a public speaking opportunity pass without creating conversational space for your slogan, and hammer it home.

Your presence on the Internet needs to be thorough and consistent. Don't let yourself be sidetracked by topics that have nothing to do with your message. Consistency, repetition, and the mental flexibility to draw any question back to your message will convey both your competence and your dedication to the voters.

◦

The race against Cohn was only the second time during his eighteen-year tenure that Workman had faced a challenger for the treasurer's office, and this probably left him unprepared for the bare-knuckle fight his opponent wanted to have. For a relatively minor position in such a small city as ours, the tone of the campaign between these septuagenarians was jarring because it was so unexpected—like two old men having a disagreement while standing in line for a movie, and one of them producing a knife.

Cohn's campaign took a no-prisoners approach that reflected the personalities of the two guys who were helping him run it. They were unrelenting political brawlers who believed the easiest way to skin a cat was to scrape its skin off the pavement after you flattened it with a Mack truck.

Although you rarely caught a glimpse of him behind the wheel, Dick Daley was Hermosa's Mack truck driver-in-chief.[1] An experienced politician himself, Daley spent two terms on the

---

1 "Dick Daley" is a pseudonym.

Hermosa Beach City Council. We served three years together in office from 2006 through 2009, and despite our political differences, Daley was instrumental in helping me win my first election. More about that later.

Daley had a keen political sense. It was uncanny. Like a handicapper at the track, he could survey candidates in the paddock and pick a winner, as he did in 2005 when he fingered a little-known Torrance city councilman named Ted Lieu to win our district's vacant assembly seat. (At the time of this writing, Lieu is in the House of Representatives, and will probably be there for many, many years.) Daley had a coldly calculating, objective eye in a field dominated by people who make decisions based on emotion and hope, and this was a rare gift. Like being able to play music by ear or match patterned shirts and striped ties, some folks are able to do it and they probably don't even know why.

Daley's political bête noire was a local political operative; let's call him Horace Blatt. When he wasn't plotting with Daley, Blatt had a campaign consulting business that specialized in political mail. Specifically, Blatt's house specialty was slate mail.

Blatt's slate mailers, like almost all slate mailers, were anything but carefully crafted political messages. The *LA Weekly* newspaper described the practice thusly: "Campaign literature tends to fall somewhere between glib hyperbole and outright deceit. Perhaps in no other area is this more evident than in the seedy world of 'slate mailers.'"

Ready to become a little more cynical about politics? The groups who purportedly publish the slate mailers are fictional, and the endorsements they offer are almost always made up. Political consultants pick titles for their mailers that will resonate with a targeted segment of the voting population. For example, women between the ages of twenty-five and forty who are likely to have school-age children will probably respond to a slate mailer titled "Education Professionals' Voter Guide." Republican voters, on the other hand, might make voting choices based on a piece of mail put out by the make-believe "Conservative Voters League."

Publishers offer to put candidates on these mailers for a fee. The more unscrupulous publishers threaten to put the opposing candidate on the mailer if a particular candidate refuses to buy a spot. At their worst, publishers tell all the candidates there are a limited number of spots and sell to the highest bidder.

Are these mailers deceptive? Well, sort of. Normally they bear some indication of which candidates paid for the spots on the slate, but that is usually in the fine print. The First Amendment of the Bill of Rights protects the right to film and sell pornography, and it also protects slate mailers, which have markedly less societal value than do skin flicks.

Slate mailers are a high-volume, low-cost way for a candidate to get his or her name in front of different segments of the voting population.

Now for the sheepish confession: (Standing up) *Hi, my name is Kit Bobko,* (Hi, Kit!) *and I've used Horace Blatt's slate mailers in the past.* (Thanks for coming, have a seat.)

Slate mailers are cheap, and the sad truth is that they work.

Dirty Politics

Daley and Blatt used their skill with political mail to great effect in 2006, when they ran Daley's wife, Lynn Olson, for a superior court judgeship. Lynn Olson was, according to an editorial in the *Los Angeles Times*, "an inactive attorney who ran Manhattan Bread & Bagel with her husband, Hermosa Beach City Council member [Dick Daley]."

In California, judges are appointed by the governor but have to stand for election every six years. Incumbent judges rarely draw a challenge, but if they do, there is an election. In the June 2006 election cycle, Daley and Blatt targeted registered Republican Superior Court Judge Dzintra Janavs. As you read that sentence, the same thought bubble probably appeared above your head that appeared above the head of virtually every voter in Los Angeles County who saw that name on the ballot: *Is Janavs a man or a woman? What kind of name is that?* Her strangely foreign, androgynous name obscured the fact that she was one of the most respected jurists in Los Angeles County, if not the state. In fact, the Boalt Hall–educated Janavs was one of only two lawyers the Los Angeles County Bar Association rated *Exceptionally Well Qualified* for the bench in that election. Olson? The Bar Association rated her *Not Qualified*.

This was politics, however, not the practice of law. Qualifications didn't matter.

Daley and Blatt knew the only thing that mattered was their target's name. Daley told me during the election in 2006 that they'd picked Janavs (the surname is Latvian; her family fled the Russians after World War II) precisely because the judge's name sounded like it was from an unknown, faraway place. Remember, June 2006 was not too far removed from September 11, 2001, and Daley and Blatt cynically bet that most red-blooded Angelenos would sooner punch their ballot for the all-American sounding Lynn Olson than they would for what-godless-corner-of-the-world-is-that-name-from Dzintra Janavs.

And they were right. Daley's wife spent $120,000 on political mailers, and the voters in Los Angeles County tossed Judge Janavs out of office, giving Olson 56 percent of the vote. According to the *Los Angeles Times*, Janavs was the first sitting judge defeated for re-election in 18 years.

So dismayed was the California State Bar that a few days after the election, then-Governor Arnold Schwarzenegger specially reappointed Janavs to the Los Angeles County Superior Court. [Insert your own *I'll be back* reference here.]

⌒

Daley and Blatt did the same political calculus for Cohn's race against Workman that they'd done with Janavs. They crafted a simple message for their candidate that they repeated over and over again: Workman had incompetently handled the city's finances for many years, and his negligence had cost Hermosa Beach millions.

Cohn sent mail to voters purporting to show that Hermosa Beach's return on its investments was much lower than that of neighboring cities. Cohn's political mail also suggested that someone competent would have done something over the last eighteen years to fix the problem.

Workman, of course, was the person Cohn and his accomplices fingered for being asleep at the fiscal switch.

Orchestrated by Daley and Blatt, Cohn's campaign was predictably effective. It also affected Workman. I saw it.

A week before the election, then-candidate Cohn came to the microphone during the public comment portion of our city council meeting and highlighted statements Workman had made at a recent candidates' forum questioning the security of the Federal Deposit Insurance Corporation (FDIC) and Bank of America.

Blatt followed his client to the microphone to sharpen and emphasize the point that Workman was fiscally incompetent, just in case anyone had missed it. The issue for the city council, said Blatt, was to come up with a policy that decided whether the city was going to keep money in banks or not. The implied premise was that Workman thought the city's money should be kept somewhere other than a bank, perhaps in shoeboxes in a locked file cabinet in the basement at city hall.

When his opponent finished, Workman, visibly agitated, rose from his seat and came to the podium. The city council chambers got quiet in the way conversations in a restaurant become whispers when a couple nearby is having an argument.

I've tried to run a good campaign without the mud, Workman said, *but you know what, I'm tired of this.* His voice rose; unconsciously he rapped his knuckles on the podium.

The innuendoes are really driving me nuts, and it's not fair and it's not honest. And as far as the deceit that's involved in all this, I don't understand. We're going to elect some of these guys? Heavens to Betsy, that frightens me to death!

Cohn and Blatt sat smugly in the audience and watched their competitor unravel live on TV. Those of us who knew Workman saw that the election had crossed a line. Cohn's unrelenting campaign and Blatt's pointed mail had struck home. The

Secret No. 1 – Know Why You Are Running

attacks reduced Workman to defending more than just his record and policy positions; he was defending his honor and himself. The man I saw speaking that night was not the man I knew. Workman was a man besieged in a political campaign that in his mind had turned into a personal referendum.

I guess it had.

At that moment, standing at the podium in the crowded city council chambers with his sniggering opponents sitting right behind him, I am certain John Workman also felt completely alone.

❦

Be prepared for dirty tricks. You know they're coming; politics is famous for them. Your opponents will find something in your past that can hurt you, or they'll just make something up. Be ready, and take them in stride.

Silver lining: They pretty much only hit you when you're a threat, or already successful. If it happens to you—and if you're in politics long enough it will—know that you're probably doing something right.

❦

On Tuesday, November 8, 2011, Hermosa Beach voters elected David Cohn as their new city treasurer. He defeated Workman 57 percent to 43 percent, receiving 1,371 votes to Workman's 1,072. There were approximately 13,000 voters in Hermosa Beach then, but on that November day, fewer than

2,500 came to the polls. It was hardly a landslide for Cohn or a clear-cut rebuke of Workman. It was a hard-fought, narrow loss.

∽

The following day, when the election was over, I called Workman. He didn't pick up his phone, so I left him a voicemail. I can't remember exactly what I said, but I know I told him how sorry I was that he had lost, and how I thought he was better off without the stress. I reminded him that he was, after all, advancing in his years and had grandchildren and a wonderful wife, and spending time with them was much better than puttering around city hall and listening to us drone on at council meetings. I told him he'd answered when the city had needed him and had served honorably for nearly twenty years. It was time for him to play more golf, or do more dancing, or take a trip to Greece. I told him he was better than what he'd just been put through.

I had a dinner event that night, and sometime during the evening Workman returned my call. He left me a voice mail. By the time I left my dinner it was late, so I planned to return his call the following day.

Workman's message thanked me for calling him, and he said many of his friends had called, but he'd stayed away from the phone for most of the day. He told me he was tremendously relieved that the campaign was over, and that it had been hard, but he felt much, much better now that it was over. He said he was going to do some of the things I suggested, and that in retrospect he shouldn't have let the silliness of the campaign bother him.

The John Workman who left me that message was perceptibly relieved, happy, and sounded like the guy I'd come to know over the past years. He sounded well.

Early the next morning, I got a phone call from my city manager telling me John Workman was gone.

He had passed during the night.

Losing Is Inevitable, but It Isn't the End

There is nothing quite so pointedly personal as losing an election, particularly when the loss means being voted out of office. The city John Workman loved and had raised his children in had turned him out. I don't think he knew it on the night it happened, but the defeat broke his heart; it was simply too much for him to bear.

When you lose—and at some point, you will—try to lose as gracefully as you can. Be classy, even when the classless beat you.

This isn't just for the sake of your own dignity. Your next election will build directly on the bones of this defeat. Remember that the people who supported you—your contributors, your volunteers, your family, and everyone who voted for you—are all watching, and they'll all remember how your character showed through in this moment of adversity. They'll remember if you smash your guitar and run off stage crying, and they'll remember if you were kind and generous to everyone who was disappointed by the night's results. And politics is circular. You'll need all those positive memories when the time comes to try again.

Look Out for Scandals

Now, almost exactly a year after my friend died, Olsen was on the phone asking me if I knew about an extortion plot involving Workman's replacement, David Cohn.

Extortion?

Cohn was, after all, a seventy-two-year-old man in questionable health who wobbled around with all the grace of a tipsy penguin. And this was Hermosa Beach, not Mexico City. Elected officials here didn't drive around in all-black Denalis with rough-looking dudes in dark suits and mirrored sunglasses in the front seat.

Olsen didn't have all the facts, because he was operating on a tip, but the story he'd been told involved Cohn and a masseuse. Actually, to be fair to the tipster and to massage professionals around the world, the aforementioned masseuse was definitely a pro . . . but of the topless, unlicensed, Craigslist variety.

People make mistakes. Every district has its share of scandals, and in most communities those scandals eventually become more or less public knowledge. As a candidate, you must be especially aware of the way they influence voters' decisions. Even the older scandals; collective memory and rumors have a way of unearthing old enemies and tugging at the strings of current events. Everyone knows whose kid got the DUI. Everyone knows whose wife was running around on him. Political circles can be close-knit, particularly in smaller districts, and these kinds of scandals matter to a certain percentage of the electorate.

By the same token, be mindful of your own past. Clean up your social media accounts long before you announce your candidacy, and settle any outstanding debts. Be careful. Be thorough. Remember that once you step into the political arena, other people will be looking for your mistakes.

⌒

Olsen's investigation led him to Yuritsi Maria Garcia, the twenty-six-year-old mother of two whom the city treasurer had found on Craigslist. According to the papers, Ms. Garcia (or "Diana," as she listed herself on Craigslist) had been working as a masseuse for several months when her relationship with Cohn began. Diana (let's use her preferred stage name) lived with her kids and her boyfriend, Gustavo Ceron, in Maywood, a largely Hispanic, working-class community in central Los Angeles County, twenty miles east of Hermosa Beach.

The treasurer was drawn to Diana's Craigslist ad because she offered deep tissue and sensual massages. Massages were not included in his company's health insurance plan (Cohn suffered from an ailing back), so he took it upon himself to find a masseuse who could provide the necessary therapy. Cohn actually said this under penalty of perjury in court.

Olsen's investigation of the relationship between Cohn and Diana revealed that it was at best sketchy, and almost certainly illegal. The blatant illegality of the relationship would also explain why the police report later released to the press was so heavily redacted; on one of the pages there were only two sentences that weren't entirely blacked out.

Between the investigative reporting and what came out in courtroom testimony, here's what is known for certain: Cohn travelled to Diana's Maywood home in late October 2012 for one of her deep tissue and sensual massages and agreed to pay her $40 for a thirty-minute session.

Everything went fine, Diana told Olsen; *he actually took a shower in my house. He was polite and respectful. He called me after the massage. He said he really liked me.* When you read those words from Olsen's story your creepy-meter also probably pegged.

Olsen also learned from his interview with Diana that her work had done the trick, and she and Cohn soon began trading text messages.

She told me she thought I was cute and that she would like to see me again, Cohn would later testify in court.

Olsen uncovered more, but the facts of the rest of the story depend largely on who is telling it. Here's what we think we know: Cohn's interest in the masseuse progressed even further over the next few days, and he sent her what the newspapers labeled an explicit video. (Imagine a shaky iPhone video of Danny DeVito trying to seduce you with his manly wiles. Let that visual sink in.) The two also exchanged a series of graphic phone calls.

About the phone calls, Diana said, *I didn't charge him.*

Until I read that in the newspaper, I thought lawyers were the only ones who charged clients for phone calls.

Mercifully, I never saw the video, but from what Olsen told me, it was distressingly explicit.

I spoke with Olsen at some point while the story was unfolding. I was curious if he or any of his editors had seen it. At the time, Cohn was still denying any wrongdoing, and I wondered if Olsen's editors would make the video public. I also knew Olsen had been to Diana's home and interviewed her. I assumed she had a copy of the video and was probably more than willing to share it in order to verify her side of the story.

So, I asked Olsen, *have you seen it?*

I have, the young reporter said.

And?

Put it this way, I don't have enough alcohol in my house to cleanse my brain of what I saw.

Anthony Weiner, step aside. Still shots of your congressional aide in all their glory have nothing on the videos made by Hermosa Beach treasurer David Cohn.

Well, I told Olsen, *I guess I'm glad we have people like you on the front lines of the news to view things like that, so the general public doesn't have to.*

That wasn't the worst of it, Olsen said. *The worst part was the audio.*

Keeping the Press Close

Knowing how to deal with the press won't mean instant victory, but it will make your life easier. The press can assist in selling your ideas, they can help you get your name out to the public, and they can shine light on issues that you can use to build your brand.

As a candidate (and eventually, a politician), you'll need to build real relationships with a handful of reporters—usually an assortment from TV, radio, print, and social media, including bloggers. These aren't people you can trust with your secrets (obviously), but some trust must exist between you. They need to trust that the information you provide is genuine and reliable, and you need to trust that information they pass to you is similarly accurate. Get to know these people. Get their contact information, and use it with some regularity. Building a working relationship with them may offset any attack pieces they may write (because they'll hate to lose a good source of information); but more important, they can be an extremely good source of information *to you*. You want to know what the press knows, so you can't afford to keep them at arm's length. But be prepared for bloggers or reporters who will seek out dirt on you or take quotes out of context. If you're in the public eye, this will almost certainly happen.

There are essentially two kinds of media: earned and unearned. For instance, if I, as chairman of the Pier Avenue Development committee, were to suddenly announce a million-dollar renovation of Hermosa Beach's main thoroughfare, it would be considered "earned" media because a reporter would be assigned to cover that story. The story has nothing to do with who I am, but because of my association with it, my name gets into the article and my reputation gets a bump.

"Unearned" media is roughly the opposite: someone calls a press conference and declares that he supports my candidacy over another guy's. This is a story that exists purely to shout my name from the rooftops. I did nothing to "earn" that press coverage.

As you will soon see with Treasurer Cohn, the saying that all press is good press (whether "earned" or "unearned") isn't necessarily true.

Sometimes press coverage isn't enough, or it's unavailable, and your next best option is social media. The demographic information provided by Facebook can be invaluable when it comes to targeting your message. Exhibit "A" for a successful social media campaign is Donald Trump, who used Twitter to bypass the press and bring his message straight to his supporters. With a lot of social media, you can't necessarily control what gets out into the Internet, and once it's gone, it's gone. Monitoring it can be a time-consuming task, but it's one you should keep an eye on. Many campaigns assign a full-time staffer to the candidate's social media accounts. All said, social media is a worthwhile tool, but like any tool, it can also be a weapon if you hold it right.

On November 3, 2012, almost exactly one year to the day after defeating Workman, Cohn invited Diana to his home for a one-hour massage. The price for her services was $100, and he promised to pay for her gas.

According to police reports, Diana arrived at Cohn's home on the appointed date at the agreed-upon hour, wearing a short black dress and small shorts. She went into Cohn's home to provide the deep tissue, sensual massage while her boyfriend waited outside in the car. What happened next was a criminal action involving the Craigslist masseuse and the Hermosa Beach city treasurer.

Diana told Olsen the massage began—as all of her massages did with Cohn—topless. Nobody involved in the massage that day was wearing a shirt. In later courtroom testimony, it came out that nobody was wearing pants either.

In her interview with Olsen, Diana said that shortly after the massage began, *He began touching me.* Diana told Olsen that Cohn asked her for sex, but this was more than she had agreed to for her $100 fee, and she refused. Diana said at that point she stopped the massage.

At the preliminary hearing in the Torrance Superior Court, Diana's testimony about the scope of her services changed. A Hermosa Beach detective who investigated the case said Diana told him she was a massage therapist who assisted in helping customers achieve sexual release or climax, and that she allowed clients to touch her naked body during the massage. More to the point, the detective testified that Diana always gave clients a happy ending. The detective said Diana tried to service Cohn during the massage, but he was, um, frustrated . . . and at that point he cut the massage short.

No happy ending here.

As expected, Cohn told a different story. Cohn testified that he disrobed and lay facedown on the floor in the guest room, but *I couldn't see everything that was going on.*

I couldn't see she was nude, Cohn said.

Apparently, unbeknownst to Cohn, who was facedown on the floor in a guest room in his own home, Diana, with catlike quietude, had disrobed.

But something was amiss, and it took Cohn only twenty minutes to assess what it was.

An *apparatus.* Cohn testified in court that *When I was lying on my stomach, I could not see what she was doing, but I think she was using some kind of apparatus.* The detective testified that

Cohn told him Diana's use of the sex toy offended his sensibilities and forced him to put an end to the proceedings.

That's what made him feel uncomfortable, the detective testified.

Not surprisingly, Diana remembered things differently. By her account, she ended the massage twenty minutes in. She said Cohn grabbed her arm and tried talking to her, but she was upset and retreated to a nearby bathroom, where she called her boyfriend, who was parked outside in the couple's 1999 Dodge minivan. The boyfriend, whom Cohn described in the police report as a *stalky [sic] built Hispanic man,* came to his girlfriend's aid and began knocking loudly on the front door.

Diana emerged from the bathroom and asked Cohn for her C-note, but he refused to pay. The massage had lasted only twenty minutes, so he offered her a discounted sum for her services—$65. Diana took the money, and because she was so obviously upset, she said Cohn also gave her his iPad. She testified that he even took a few minutes to show her how to use it.

Cohn remembered events differently. According to him, he was distracted by the loud knocking, and while he was thinking about what to say to the *stalky built Hispanic man* banging on his front door, Diana took the opportunity to nick his iPad. He only noticed it was missing after she left, and he said he called her repeatedly asking that she return it.

About a week later Diana responded to Cohn's pleas and agreed to delete the contents of the iPad, but said that she would keep the device. She also demanded that Cohn deposit $6,000 into one of her accounts, and if he didn't pay by the end of the week, the price would increase to $10,000. Cohn testified under oath that Diana had threatened to release private photos of his family to the public if he failed to make the deposit. Diana also specified that she wanted the money put directly into her account because she was worried about Cohn paying her with counterfeit bills. She had only known our treasurer for a short time, but the Craigslist masseuse definitely knew her man.

Recognizing that the situation had spiraled out of his control, and wanting his iPad and whatever photos it contained returned, Cohn notified the Hermosa Beach police about his predicament the Monday after his massage gone wrong. When asked in court why he had waited over the weekend to file a report with the police, Cohn said he'd wanted to wait until *the proper people were there* for him to speak to. Presumably, the *proper people* included the city's interim police chief.

On November 8, 2012, five days after the incident, Cohn contacted a Hermosa Beach detective and showed him the text message exchanges. The text messages never became public, but the treasurer said Diana had threatened to release pictures of his family to city staff.

We are a private family, and those pictures don't go out to anybody, Cohn said.

꩜

The police and Cohn set up a sting to catch Diana at the bank. Cohn told his masseuse to go to her bank in Maywood and he would meet her there with the money.

She went, but the only thing she got were *Miranda* rights when the police arrested her.

He just set me up, Diana said after her arrest. *I never thought he would do that.*

The detectives recovered the iPad, which, interestingly, had already had its contents remotely erased by Apple. *It was as if it was a brand new iPad,* according to the detective in charge of the investigation.

So then why all the fuss? What was Cohn so concerned would be released to the press or posted on the Internet? These questions were never answered. One can only speculate as to why.

The Hermosa Beach police arrested Diana on November 8, 2012, and when they did she filed a sexual assault charge against Cohn.

Minding the Fallout

Like everyone else in town, I was reading with increasing concern about Cohn's problems. Felony extortion didn't happen to city treasurers often—and it never happened in Hermosa Beach. I thought it best that Cohn take a leave of absence while things got sorted out.

Making matters worse, *L'affair Cohn* occurred just as the treasurer had unilaterally decided to shop the city's funds to a new bank of his choosing, and he had jealously refused to allow the city council or finance director to participate in the selection process.

This bothered me, but it was deeply worrying to my city council colleague—let's call him Boyd Goodfellow—who had the same misgivings about Cohn that I did. I don't remember that we ever spoke about it, but somehow we arrived at the same conclusion: that something about the waddling red-nosed financier was half a bubble off of level.

I remember one meeting in which Goodfellow told me he'd asked Cohn what he was doing with the public's funds—because he and the public had a right to know. Instead of promising to chat with the city councilman, Cohn flatly rebuffed the inquiry.

You're barking up the wrong tree, buddy, he told Goodfellow over one shoulder, and doddered away.

Over the course of the following months, Goodfellow continued to ask questions about the treasurer's activities, and Cohn continued to invite the city councilman to pound sand.

The issue devolved to the point where Goodfellow was forced to request the e-mail between Cohn, his assistant, and the banks he was soliciting for proposals through the same legal process any member of the public would. Cohn had steadfastly refused to cooperate otherwise.

When the e-mail was finally produced, we found that Cohn had used five different e-mail accounts for communicating with the banks and city staff, and none of the e-mails had come from his personal or city e-mail accounts. Who has five active e-mail accounts anyway? (At least he didn't have his own server.) That seemed strange. No, it seemed suspicious.

Coupled with a felony extortion plot against him, Cohn's multiplicity of e-mail accounts and his smug reluctance to share what he'd been doing went from merely troubling to downright frightening. Remember, those of us on the city council were learning the facts at the same rate Olsen was uncovering them.

⁓

Adding to the general consternation around city hall was the fact that the only things we heard from Cohn weren't actually from Cohn himself. His newly hired criminal defense attorney periodically issued bland, carefully tailored statements on his client's behalf. Meanwhile, a nervous city staff assured us that no sensitive information had been compromised in the massage gone wrong, but shouldn't we take every possible precaution with the public's money? It seemed clear that Cohn's duty to the city was to step aside and let folks unconnected to his office ensure that nothing untoward had gone on while he was in it.

On November 25, 2012, Goodfellow and I coauthored a letter asking for Cohn's resignation, or at least that he take a leave of absence and attend to his personal affairs, which now included a tawdry case playing out in the Torrance Superior Court.

Our request was just good government and was no different from what you'd do in your own business if the same situation arose. If nothing else, it would give the city a chance to focus on something else for a while, because the scandal was consuming an inordinate amount of attention from everyone involved. In a small city like Hermosa Beach, there are only so many people to handle the city's business. Things don't get done if everyone is focused on cleaning up a mess. I imagine the same thing is true at all levels of government.

The editorial staff at Olsen's newspaper agreed. The paper published an editorial calling for the city council to put Cohn on leave *to protect the integrity of the city* because regardless of how this fiasco finally turned out, *it isn't likely to have a happy ending.*

Even serious newsmen can't help themselves sometimes.

∽

On Monday, May 6, 2013, Cohn turned in his letter of resignation to the Hermosa Beach city clerk. Cohn's letter said he *had taken on more responsibilities than one at this stage of life should do*. The letter went on to say he was too busy with teaching and work to devote his full attention to his new position with the city.

Those words must have been cold comfort to John Workman's family.

There had been backroom negotiations going on for some time between city staff and Cohn about whether he should remain in office, and he gradually became convinced it was time to move on. I was pleased at his decision because I couldn't imagine the effort that would have been involved in keeping an eye on him for the three years remaining in his term. I just flat-out didn't trust the man, and this was a problem for someone whose main job was keeping track of the city's money.

Whatever happened to Diana and her boyfriend? At their arraignment, the two pleaded not guilty to the felony extortion charges against them. Diana served 8 days, and her boyfriend Mr. Ceron was sentenced to 160 days in county jail and three years' probation.

No charges were ever brought against Cohn for sexual assault.

SECRET No. 2
Get Comfortable Asking for Money

Asking for Money

Kit, we have a problem.

I had just finished giving my first-ever speech at a fundraiser, and things had gone pretty well. I'd hit my marks and delivered what I thought was a compelling message about why the audience should give me their votes—and their dollars.

Asking for money—the "mother's milk of politics," as famous California Democratic politician Jesse "Big Daddy" Unruh described it—is a daunting proposition. Aside from the cultural taboos concerning talking about money, if you want people to contribute to your campaign, you have to sell them a vision of the future that they not only want, but also believe you can provide. That kind of salesmanship takes a special kind of person, one whose devotion to a cause trumps adherence to social norms, self-doubt, and the cynicism of political opponents and naysayers. Moreover, that devotion must be strong enough to bear up under the weight of a campaign's expenses, which can be significant.

You can't be an introvert. You have to put yourself into the public eye, which means attending local events, building relationships with community leaders and influencers, and demonstrating the kind of character and effort that makes people want to invest. It's hard work. The good news, though, is that with each fundraising event, you get an opportunity to build and solidify support within your community. Fundraisers are never just about money.

Planning a fundraiser is essentially planning a public-spirited party. It should be the sort of event that broadcasts your vision for the community and indicates your involvement with prominent citizens, while also communicating your personality and approachability. Winning the support of a local business is a mutually beneficial coup: If you hold your fundraiser at a coffee shop, for example, you can serve local coffees or snacks while the coffee shop wins more customers. If you're a sports enthusiast, plan the fundraiser around a championship game. If you own a small business, persuade your fellow business owners to showcase your candidacy at their shops. One prominent Orange County politician celebrates his birthday party at a BBQ that doubles as his annual fundraiser.

Your first fundraisers should feel personal and communal at the same time. It can feel like a hard tightrope to walk, but people *will* help you. Gather together the people who will support you. Inspire them to bring their friends.

Your fundraising goal should be well defined—clear enough that you know how many events you'll need to hold before you reach that goal. So long as your events are well attended, buzz will build, and your campaign will be on its way.

As your campaign progresses, you'll find yourself working toward specific targets, and the tone of the fundraisers will shift to accommodate those new goals. If you're less worried about money and are just trying to get in front of voters, the event is usually called a coffee meeting or a house meeting. Ask supporters in different parts of town to host the coffee meetings and invite their neighbors. Such events are all about letting the voters get a look at you, hopefully so they come away thinking that you're much nicer or smarter or more approachable than they thought you were. Those functions tend to be pretty small, maxing out at around twelve people. Make no mistake: even if you're self-funding, you cannot win an election without hosting these events. No election has ever been won on mailers alone.

Having a draw for your fundraisers obviously helps.

When I started my first political campaign, I invited my uncle, a former astronaut, down from the Bay Area to help me at my first big fundraiser. I was the headliner, but he was the main attraction. A few folks might have been willing to listen to me, but lots more would come if they first got to listen to an astronaut speak about flying the space shuttle.

The combination worked, and we managed to get about fifty people in the room, some of whom brought $250 checks with them. That was the maximum amount they could contribute to my campaign under Hermosa Beach's campaign finance ordinance. The fundraiser was a success.

Or at least I thought it was . . . until just a few minutes after the event ended.

What's wrong? I asked the unimpressed curator of the space where we held our event, an art gallery in a converted old theater in downtown Hermosa Beach, formerly known as The Bijou.

On this particular night, the pieces of art featured in the gallery were large, bright, textured, monochromatic paintings. Each painting had acrylic swirled in various patterns. The paint had the consistency and appearance of wet cake frosting. There were small paintings with intricate, symmetrical curlicues and larger ones as tall as a man with three- and four-inch swirls that looked like they had been made with a trowel. All the pieces had a sheen to them because the acrylic was so thick that it was not yet dry. I was told the paint would not dry for many, many years.

These Southern California beach-chic Zen paintings were indisputably beautiful. But more than that, they were expensive. Nothing in the gallery had a price on it; if someone wished to purchase a piece they would have to do what the little tag beneath each painting instructed: *Inquire*.

That inquiry would be made with the curator. She was a woman who, up until now, had gracefully tolerated my *hoi polloi* supporters being packed into her gallery to raise money for my city council race. From the look on her face, I could see that her tolerance, and my grace period, had ended.

I need to show you something, she said.

The speeches were over, and people were talking in small groups around the room. Many crowded around my uncle, who answered questions about piloting the space shuttle and opined about the chances of putting a man on Mars. The curator walked me toward the gallery's wall, near one of the chafing dishes used by the event's caterers.

That's when I saw it: The wall, which was as white as the Pope's hat, had a trace of banana yellow acrylic paint smeared on it. Nothing big, but the color contrast to the rest of the white wall was unmistakable. Yellow. Right there. It stood out like a fly in milk, if the fly were bright yellow.

The curator walked a few steps further. More yellow. I could now see that there was a broader smear, like a happy dog with a yellow tail had wagged its way down the wall. Following the trail to a large, deep-sea blue painting, the serious woman with her severe ponytail stopped and pointed.

My eyes beat her to the spot. Yellow. The painting was as big as a bay window, and some of the blue swirls along the very bottom had newly applied bright yellow acrylic on their tips.

This is a problem, she said.

Sure it was. And I had no idea what to do about it. My first instinct was the one my mother had taught my brothers and me whenever she took us someplace with delicate things little boys might be inclined to touch: *You break it, you buy it.*

So, because my mom raised us right, I asked, *How much does this piece cost?*

Maybe I could write her a check, I thought, and add something new to my living room. None of my friends would know the yellow along the bottom edge was a late, unintended addition. Maybe I could hide that part behind the couch. But her one-word response nearly stopped my heart.

Thousands, she said.

Mine was not the inquiry she had been hoping for. This was not art that would be hanging in my living room anytime soon.

My fundraiser had suddenly turned from a success into an expensive game of Clue. Instead of trying to figure out if the culprit was the butler in the parlor with a wrench, I had to figure out who had done it in the gallery with yellow acrylic paint on their *culo*.

Spending Your Money Wisely

As a candidate, your fundraising ability is critical to the overall success of a campaign, but without a campaign treasurer, it will inevitably be lost in the weeds of campaign financing laws. Watergate ushered in an era of increased scrutiny for campaign contributions; now every district and city has its own regulations governing campaign finance reporting. This is not something you can afford to overlook.

Some cities limit contributions by amount—you can only raise a certain dollar amount per contributor—while others limit the types of contributions you can raise. You might be able to raise only personal contributions in one city, but in the next one, you're allowed to take money from corporations as well as private citizens. The sheer complexity of the subject requires you to be smart . . . and hire a professional. Slipping up can result in you being audited or fined (or worse), and hiring a professional campaign treasurer can keep your campaign safe and functional.

A campaign treasurer should know the specific rules your city expects you to abide by. They will know the nitty-gritty details of how to get a campaign ID number and which kind of bank account will best serve your needs while complying with your city's regulations. The whole purpose of a treasurer is to keep your campaign on the rails and to take care of the little things that can push you off track before they become a problem.

Once you've recruited a campaign treasurer, the next step is to draft a finance plan with reachable goals. This finance plan will include fundraising goals and a budget, which should track income and expenditures (the latter should be kept as low as possible).

Secret No. 2 – Get Comfortable Asking for Money

Your fundraising should start with a list of fifty people who can contribute the maximum amount to your campaign (think family, friends, and colleagues). Call them first. These people are a sort of test balloon for how much support you're likely to win in the community overall—after all, if you can't get your family and friends to give you their hard-earned money, the likelihood that you'll win strangers to your side and convince them to contribute is pretty slim.

Support and name recognition are connected, but winning money and spending money are separate things, and once you've got a good chunk of change, figuring out the most strategic way to spend it can spell the difference between a campaign that flies and one that crashes and burns.

Here's a list of what campaigns usually spend money on:

- ✓ Mailers
- ✓ Staff (treasurer and campaign manager)
- ✓ Website and social media
- ✓ Walking material (i.e., brochures and other handouts)
- ✓ Yard signs
- ✓ Photo shoots
- ✓ Robocalls (automated telephone calls)
- ✓ Stickers, buttons, and hats to identify you and your volunteers
- ✓ Local commercials (if your district is big enough)
- ✓ Polling

Your budget may not extend to everything, and it should go without saying that if you can't afford it, don't spend your money on it. The first three items—mailers, staff, and social media—are the most effective, and ergo, the most important. Don't scrimp on them.

Candidates provide the lawn signs to their supporters so they can show their neighbors whom they plan to vote for on Election Day. Or that's what candidates think.

A veteran political consultant once told me the yard sign's only purpose was to make a candidate feel good. Other than that, I was told, the signs were worthless, expensive clutter. Have you ever seen a sign in someone's front yard and *because of that sign* reconsidered your opinion of the candidate? No. That's not something people do. Lawn signs aren't an effective way to change minds, so spending money on them is wildly inefficient—no matter how much they stroke the candidate's ego.

The most effective way to spend money is on voter contact, which, historically, has been through the mail. About 40 percent of your budget should go to mailers. You're probably going to want to send out several different mailers, highlighting different campaign issues or aspects of yourself to appeal to different demographics. To do this, you'll need to work out the number of high-propensity voters (voters who regularly vote every two years) and find out what they care about, and then you'll need to frame your message in such a way as to speak to their concerns. This kind of research is essential ground game and can, to some extent, be done during the everyday events of your campaign. Remember, fundraising is never just about money!

As time presses on, campaign strategies must adapt to new social pressures and opportunities. Social media is likely to play a larger role in the voter contact process, particularly since electronic campaign messages are cheaper than mailers and can be tracked by the campaign. Moreover, the way that people find and consume information has changed dramatically, a shift that means the rules for campaigning are themselves changing with each election cycle.

What's in a Name?
The three most important things that win elections are name recognition, name recognition, and name recognition. Name recognition is the point of fundraisers, as it's hard to build name recognition without funding, and name recognition is *the* thing that wins elections. You've seen the boost that it gives to celebrities like Arnold Schwarzenegger, Clint Eastwood, and Donald Trump. Qualifications and policy positions cannot compete with sheer name familiarity, even in local politics.

You don't have to be a national superstar to find fame useful. Small-scale fame within a community can give you a big boost and be a launching pad for success. Are you a beloved athlete? Or maybe an influential teacher? Someone who knows every parent whose kid passed through the school? Being plugged into a community institution can garner goodwill as well as name recognition.

If you're going to run for office, you must recognize that you aren't simply running for your own sake. The job of a democratically elected official will always be tied up in representing the will of the voters. If you can't match the will of the voters—if most people straight up disagree with you or feel you don't match the character of the town—run in a different district.

The character of a town is something you can actually see by just taking a stroll through the streets. I'm not talking about architecture or how well public flower beds are maintained; it's the style of the residents themselves that will tell you the preferred style of their elected officials. For instance, in entrepreneurial cities like Orange, California, it's not uncommon for people to attend city council meetings in their Sunday best. But in laid-back Hermosa Beach, if you appear at a city council meeting in a three-piece suit, people will know you're not a local. I got much further with people when I lost the formality and showed up in board shorts and flip-flops. A good candidate looks like the people he or she is trying to represent. It is a visual indication that he or she already knows what issues are important to the city.

And you do need to know what those issues are. You need to be aware of what matters to people. Once you fully understand the needs and character of your electorate, you can clearly state your values, your reasons for running, and the exact things you want to achieve. Weave those two perspectives together into a compelling message that calls people to action.

But while you're busy turning yourself into a conduit for the people, you can't forget the individual history that makes up the person you've always been. That person is complex and interesting—but also vulnerable. A lifetime of possible mistakes will come back to bite you when you run for office, so define yourself in the public eye before your opponents can.

For example, it may be a good idea to empty the skeletons in your closet (i.e., bankruptcies, divorces, arrests, etc.) and spin them in a favorable light before your opponents can portray you in a way that benefits them. If you allow other people to tell your truths, you lose control of the story. I'd been in the military for years and had never gotten to choose where I wanted to live, so when I first ran for office, my opponents accused me of being a "carpetbagger." I was eventually able to explain my military background and consequent lack of roots in the community, and I was able to articulate why I'd chosen Hermosa Beach as my home. (Senator John McCain, a Navy pilot held as a POW for almost six years in Vietnam, famously quashed the allegation that he was a "carpetbagger" when he first ran for office by explaining that the longest he'd ever lived anywhere before Arizona was in Hanoi.) I won in part because I was eventually able to take their accusations and turn them into a sympathetic and easily understandable talking point, but not every accusation has such a harmless outcome.

Defining yourself means embracing all the parts of your upbringing and heritage that might appeal to your electorate, including race, religion, and educational background. To some extent, this may mean acknowledging something that has no obvious payoff: I'm half-Spanish and I received the endorsement of California GROW Elect, an organization focused on electing Latino Republicans in California . . . but there aren't that many Latinos in Hermosa Beach! I'm certain that my Spanish heritage would have had more impact if I'd been campaigning in certain parts of Los Angeles, but because I was in Hermosa Beach, it only went so far. But you know what? Every little bit helps, and you can't hold anything back. Campaigns are brutal, and just like any other ultracompetitive endeavor, it will take every piece of you to win. But in the end—provided you don't exaggerate—honesty and self-awareness will protect you.

∽

If money is the mother's milk of politics—and it is—name recognition is a very close second. For example, a popular mayor who decides to run for higher office may be well known in his city, but the people in the next town over probably have no idea who he is. A candidate's positions on the issues are important, but if voters don't know who you are, it's unlikely they'll vote for you, no matter where you stand.

Overcoming the name-recognition issue is a real problem, even for the best first-time candidates. My friend Dan Adler is a great example of this.

Adler was one of the Democratic candidates when I ran for Congress in 2011. It didn't take long, sitting with him at debates, to see he was the kind of person we all hope will choose to serve in public office. Adler was a Hollywood insider, and an articulate, thoughtful, thoroughly likable guy. If I hadn't been in the race myself, Adler would have won my vote.

But as smart and well informed as he was, Adler's main problem was that the voters in our district couldn't pick him out of a lineup. They certainly couldn't pick him out of a lineup that included well-known Democratic politicians, such as Los Angeles City councilwoman (now LA County Supervisor) Janice Hahn; California Secretary of State Debra Bowen; and left-wing, anti-war darling Marcy Winograd.

Secret No. 2 – Get Comfortable Asking for Money

Adler attempted to overcome this problem like anyone in Hollywood would: He called on his famous friends for help. Grammy Award winner Macy Gray had an impromptu concert for him. He also shot a series of clever and very funny TV commercials with his campaign manager, actor Sean Astin.

But as clever as his TV spots were, and despite all the famous people he had campaigning with him, Adler still only managed to garner a small percentage of the votes on Election Day. He simply didn't have enough money or time to overcome his anonymity with the voters in our district.

When I ran for city council for the first time in 2005, I had the exact same problem. Hermosa Beach voters didn't know me from Adam. I didn't know actors like Sean Astin who could shoot cool TV spots for me, nor did I have singers like Macy Gray who could make catchy campaign ads for me.

But I did have an astronaut in the family.

Negative Advertising

My introduction to Hermosa Beach politics was the November 2003 city council race, in which a local politician—let's call him Big Bobby—sought his fourth four-year term.

Big Bobby was a Republican, and his opponent in that race was Dick Daley. They served together on the Hermosa Beach City Council a few years later and didn't much care for each other, at least not politically.

Daley was a Chicago-style Democrat who brought the Windy City's political approach with him to Southern California. Plainspoken and unassuming in manner, Daley's Midwestern pragmatism normally kept him from wasting his political clout on symbolic gestures—unless the symbolism moved him closer to a political goal. He didn't have a thirst for the spotlight, and as a politician, that made him both effective and dangerous. Effective because he only cared about the result, and dangerous because you probably weren't going to see him coming.

Big Bobby was Daley's polar opposite. He was a big, jovial, Boston-bred lawyer who genuinely enjoyed public life and everything that went with it. Big Bobby was a registered Republican, had a quick wit, and was keenly aware he was a public figure. There was never any doubt whether Big Bobby was in the room, and if the people in that room were polled, there would be a clear division of opinion about him. People either loved him or hated him, and Big Bobby didn't seem to care much either way. On occasion he would lead with his chin; he wasn't afraid to take a punch, and he certainly knew how to deliver one. And when it came to punches, he never passed on a chance to take a poke at Daley.

Events beget events, and the rivalry between Daley and Big Bobby tipped over the first domino that ultimately led to me making fundraising speeches at the Bijou Theater in May 2006. (A month later, June 2006, the last domino in that line fell when I defeated my opponent, Cliff Clouseau, and won a seat on the city council.)

I had moved to the city after finishing law school in 2001, and I was becoming accustomed to the ubiquitous lawn signs that would pop up around October in election years. But in the months leading up to the November 2003 election, I saw something I had not seen before: lawn signs that were against Big Bobby. The plain, white signs had *BOBBY* printed on them in bold, black capitals, and *BOBBY* was circled with a large, red X through it.

Secret No. 2 – Get Comfortable Asking for Money

The signs were doubly conspicuous because they stood alone. People normally wouldn't pay to print signs opposing a particular candidate in a multi-candidate race without proposing an alternative on the same sign, or at least on another nearby. Not here. These signs were clear and unequivocal: vote for anyone *but* Big Bobby. Lawn signs are expensive, but whoever had printed these didn't much care about the election's outcome as long as it didn't result in the reelection of the big, boisterous Beantown lawyer.

Was Daley involved in any of this? Only the Shadow knows.

The race in 2003 became so contentious that when it was over, Big Bobby filed a defamation suit against Daley's colleague and political operative Horace Blatt. According to the court papers, Big Bobby alleged Blatt was responsible for putting out false mailers and making misleading phone calls on the eve of the election that cost him votes and subjected him to the "ridicule, hatred, and contempt" of his fellow residents. Big Bobby asked the court for $1 million in damages from Blatt. The judge tossed out Big Bobby's lawsuit and ordered him to pay Blatt's legal fees. Big Bobby ended up scratching a check to Blatt for $45,000, confirming much of what the mailers had said about him. Big Bobby, of course, never forgot any of this.

Blatt's mailers and the anti-Bobby lawn signs weren't quite enough to deny Big Bobby his fourth term on the city council. He won . . . barely. The candidate who finished in third in the two-seat race was Gurney Frinks, who lost by a margin smaller than most pick-up basketball games—seven votes.

In 2005, Gurney Frinks would go on to win by a wide margin the seat he'd narrowly lost in November 2003, but a tragic turn of events kept him from taking his seat on the city council after that win.

The People in Your Corner Matter
I first ran for city council in November 2005, in the same three-seat cycle with Dick Daley, who was running for his second term, and another longtime member of the city council—let's call him Joe Kozlowski—who was running for his fourth. The third member of the city council whose seat was up that cycle decided not to run for reelection, leaving a vacancy I hoped to fill.

Novice though I was, I knew enough to realize I didn't have any real expectation to unhorse Daley or Kozlowski, but I thought I might have a puncher's chance at the empty third seat. If nothing else, I thought, I could out-hustle the rest of the field.

Hustling meant enlisting the support of someone who already had weight in the community. Sometimes you'll find a former elected official or prominent community leader who can help you expand your network or make requests of the community that might sound strange coming from you. Friends and family should always be your first call, followed by people in your church, your neighborhood, or your kids' school. The more people you meet with, the more likely you are to find people who'll advocate for you.

For me, one of those people was Alonzo (not his real name), a wealthy Hermosa Beach resident who owned a chain of restaurants up and down the Southern California coast. Alonzo's restaurant was one of the first at the Pier Plaza in Hermosa Beach, and its success had made it almost synonymous with our city. Sometimes when I told people I was from Hermosa Beach, they would say, *Oh, I've been there! I had a great night once at Alonzo's!*

Secret No. 2 – Get Comfortable Asking for Money

Alonzo enjoyed a level of success that most restaurateurs can only dream about, but he had his detractors. The local Hermosa Beach prohibitionists attributed everything bad that happened on the city's plaza to Alonzo's restaurant: the crowds, the noise, the late-night activity. So powerful was the pull of Alonzo's restaurant that even high-ranking politicians sometimes succumbed. Once at a fundraiser I met the governor of a neighboring state who, when told I was the mayor of Hermosa Beach, started telling me a story about a night some years prior spent in my town when the governor worked for the airlines. I felt compelled to cut off the governor before anything too sensitive was disclosed. Had the story progressed, I'm sure the scene of the governor's youthful indiscretions might have been traced to Alonzo's establishment. Whatever the story was, both of us would be better off if I didn't know it. But that was Hermosa Beach. It was hard to find anyone who had visited who didn't have fond memories of it. And like the governor's, some memories were fonder than others!

By disposition and interest, Alonzo was a Republican, but he understood his success meant staying in the good graces of the politicians who governed the cities where he had restaurants, whatever their political stripe. Time and experience had taught him that in smaller cities, like Hermosa Beach, his prosperity was in the hands of a constantly shifting group of fickle city council members. If one elected official decided Alonzo's restaurant wasn't a good neighbor, that it was too loud at night, that it wasn't contributing enough in business taxes, or that it used too much Styrofoam, then Alonzo's business suffered. Alonzo was always looking to make and keep friends in the local government.

Alonzo came to my aid in 2006 because he knew I was a pro-business candidate, and that my opponent, noted prohibitionist Cliff Clouseau, was not. Like all politicians, I'd like to think Alonzo wanted me to win because I inspired him, or because I displayed leadership he admired, but I know I was just the better of the two competing alternatives.

What I didn't realize at the beginning of the campaign was that Gurney Frinks was sure to capture the vacant third seat. He had come within a gnat's behind of winning the last election and had the advantage over everyone else in the race of having just run for office. Hermosa residents knew his name, and nearly two thousand had cast ballots for him less than two years prior. In November 2005, Gurney Frinks had name recognition.

Gurney Frinks had also managed to secure Big Bobby's endorsement for the November 2005 election. Two former competitors in a photo-finish race were now putting the past behind them and joining together for the good of the community, and to the public, this probably looked like an act of incredible magnanimity and statesmanship. Although there may have been some truth to this, their postbellum alliance was more likely a calculation that served both of their immediate political interests. Gurney Frinks wanted Big Bobby's voters and needed to secure his endorsement to get them. Big Bobby, in turn, wanted to support the person with the best chance of defeating Dick Daley. His support of Gurney Frinks was no more complicated than that.

Churchill once said, "If Hitler invaded Hell I would make at least a favourable reference to the Devil in the House of Commons." Big Bobby was applying the same principle here.

By supporting Gurney Frinks, Big Bobby was making a safe bet that would probably yield him the vote he needed for a majority on the city council. Even if Dick Daley won a seat on the city council, Big Bobby would hold the votes necessary to foil whatever Daley wanted to do for at least the next two years.

Joining me as another first-time candidate in the November 2005 field was Cliff Clouseau. It was his first foray into electoral politics, although he had something of a history in Democratic circles and a reputation in town prior to announcing his candidacy. Cliff Clouseau's main claim to fame, as he would tell you, was his work to ban herbicides from Hermosa Beach's green belt.

The green belt is a twenty-yard-wide strip of trees and grass that runs the length of Hermosa Beach from its northern border with Manhattan Beach to the southern border with Redondo. The land was previously owned by the Santa Fe Railroad, back when a train track connected our city to the Redondo Beach harbor and greater Los Angeles to the north. Hermosa Beach purchased the land from the railroad in the 1980s, planted trees, landscaped it, and put a walking path where the tracks used to be. The green belt soon became a beautiful and popular walking path for Hermosa residents.

When the green belt became Hermosa Beach city property, the city became responsible for its landscaping and maintenance, which attracted Cliff Clouseau's ire.

According to Clouseau, the Public Works Department was using pesticides to kill weeds on the green belt, and it was absolutely unacceptable for an environmentally conscious city like Hermosa Beach to expose people (especially children) and dogs to herbicides. Cliff Clouseau mobilized the city's nascent group of environmentalists (more about them in coming chapters) to stop the practice of spraying toxins on the green belt.

Cliff Clouseau got a cool reception from the city council, not because they opposed the idea, but because they weren't sure he was upset about an actual problem. One of the councilmen—let's call him Boris—was an engineer with a technical background, and he also knew his way around the periodic table of elements. At one of the meetings at which Clouseau railed against the so-called herbicides being used on the green belt, Boris produced a jug of the stuff the Public Works Department sprayed on the weeds and read its chemical components to the audience. There were only a handful. The one component in the liquid other than water was NaCl, more commonly called by its generic name—salt. Boris gleefully—and correctly—asked Cliff Clouseau to confirm that he was standing before the city council, incensed about the city's landscapers using salt water to kill weeds on the green belt.

Cliff Clouseau was not amused by the continuing joke that it was an odd choice for someone who thought salt water was a poison to live so close to an ocean full of it. Nevertheless, to appease the people who believed this was harmful to children and pets, the city council acquiesced and stopped using it.

When the votes were tallied on November 8, 2005, Dick Daley finished first with 18 percent of the votes cast, Gurney Frinks finished second with almost 15 percent, and Joe Kozlowski was just a fraction behind him in third. Cliff Clouseau finished fourth with 13 percent, and I was fifth with 10 percent. I trailed Cliff Clouseau by about four hundred votes.

A few days after the election I heard that Gurney Frinks was not going to take the seat he'd just won. I didn't have the details,

Secret No. 2 – Get Comfortable Asking for Money

but I knew it must be something serious to prevent Gurney Frinks from realizing his goal, especially after the last election, where he'd missed winning by just a handful of votes.

I soon learned that Gurney Frinks' wife had been diagnosed with a terminal brain tumor. He immediately abandoned his city council seat to devote himself to his family. Sadly, within a few weeks she was gone.

The seat Gurney Frinks won in November 2005 was vacant. This left Dick Daley and Big Bobby in their antebellum election stalemate, and in a race to see who could fill the third seat with an ally and secure the council majority for the next two years.

The first way to fill the vacancy was for the elected council members to appoint someone to stand in for the remainder of Gurney Frinks' four-year term. This was how Big Bobby and a man we'll call The Man Who Shakes His Head (TMWSHH)—the two Republicans on the city council—wanted to fill the seat. The rationale for filling the seat via appointment was that the city had just finished an election and there was no reason to put the electorate and city to more expense when the voters' fourth choice was so clear. Cliff Clouseau finished 400 votes better than the fifth-place finisher (me), and it made sense to appoint him.

We have a fourth-place finisher who came in close to the pack of three, Big Bobby told the local paper. *I hope we don't engage in the usual politics, and we just appoint the next guy and get on with the business of the city.*[2]

The other way to fill the vacancy was by holding a special election. This was what the two Democrats on the city council, Daley and Kozlowski, wanted to do.

---
2 Robb Fulcher, "Election winner won't take council seat," *Easy Reader* (Nov. 24, 2005).

Kozlowski and Daley's reason for holding an election was equally compelling. This was the full, unexpired term, and the people should decide whom they wanted to serve, not four members of the city council. The election, Kozlowski and Daley argued, was not expensive in the grand scheme of things, and respecting the electorate's desire was worth the cost.

I think the people like to exercise their right to elect public officials, Daley told the press.

Those were the rhetorical reasons for each side's position. But as is usually the case in politics, the Machiavellian calculations for each side's preferences were a much more accurate picture of what was really going on.

Of the four sitting council members, Kozlowski was the least ideological and most independent. He was a cautious man and sometimes shied away from Big Bobby's more aggressive and controversial ideas. This meant he often ended up casting his vote with Dick Daley, who was almost always opposed to Big Bobby on issues of consequence. But Kozlowski thought for himself, so he and Daley had a loose alliance that depended on the issues—think of the US and France.

Big Bobby and TMWSHH, on the other hand, had a sponsor-client relationship—think of the Soviet Union and Cuba. TMWSHH was a decent enough guy, but on the more complex and sophisticated issues I always had the feeling he knew he was in over his head. This led to nodding, head-shaking, and useless platitudes, which frustrated his colleagues. To state it charitably, whenever TMWSHH recognized that someone else had a better grasp on whatever issue was at hand, he was content to follow along behind them. To state it less charitably, as Churchill once described his political rival Stanley Baldwin, TMWSHH was a "political pillow who always bore the imprint of the last person to sit on him." Big Bobby was normally the guy doing the sitting, and this kept TMWSHH a reliable vote for whatever he wanted to accomplish (or prevent Dick Daley from accomplishing).

This left the fifth seat on the council as the coveted swing vote, and both pairs were interested in making sure they put the candidate most favorable to them in it. Big Bobby didn't want to give Daley's choice for the vacancy, whoever it was, a chance to win. Daley and Kozlowski supported me. By extension, this meant Big Bobby didn't want me to win, which meant he put his support behind Cliff Clouseau.

It was probably more accurate to say Kozlowski and Daley supported me *and* did not want Cliff Clouseau to win. As Democrats, both had watched their comrade in action in the local Beach Cities Democratic Club, and had taken measure of the man. They had seen enough from him to know he wasn't going to be a welcome addition, and they pledged their help to make sure I defeated him.

The way the special election broke was quite remarkable. The two Democrats who were familiar with Cliff Clouseau were actively working against him because they knew who he was and what he stood for. To prevent Cliff Clouseau winning a seat, they supported the conservative Republican in the race—me. The two Republicans, on the other hand, in order to oppose their two Democratic colleagues and find a reliable third vote, backed one of the most hard-core liberal Democrats in Hermosa Beach.

I won the special election against Cliff Clouseau with Kozlowski's and Daley's support, and ironically, I always had a much closer relationship with the two Democrats than I ever did with Big Bobby and TMWSHH.

Strange bedfellows, my enemy's enemy is my friend, and all that. The one important thing to remember about political clichés is that they're clichés because they're usually true. They certainly were in this case.

Back to the Gallery...

Most people have never met an Oh-My-Goodness-You-Have-Actually-Been-In-Space astronaut face-to-face. So, as soon as Blatt (my campaign consultant—remember, I was working closely with Daley in 2006) learned that I had one in the family, he insisted that we hold a fundraising event with him. Blatt knew people would want to meet my uncle, but he also knew that an astronaut visiting Hermosa Beach would be a newsworthy event. Cold-eyed political operative that he was, Blatt saw an opportunity to kill two political birds with the one intergalactic stone; a campaign event with my uncle would increase my name recognition with voters and raise money.

Admittedly, all this was new to me because I'd never thought of my uncle as anyone other than just my uncle. I'd grown up in the Air Force. My middle brother and I were born on Air Force bases, and we both graduated from the Air Force Academy, just like my father and uncle. Some of my first memories are of my mom hustling me into the backyard in time to see my pop's fighter jet fly over the house. I knew which plane in the formation was his because he waggled the wings when they were overhead. I remember going with my dad to Kings Island as a boy, and being afraid of the park's signature rollercoaster—The Beast. As we stood in line, my dad must have sensed my trepidation about the ride. My anxiety increased as we shuffled closer to the front of the line and watched as the cars clinked up the incline and dropped over the top in a whoosh. Right before it was our turn, and to no one in particular, the fighter pilot observed the big drop was *only half the angle of attack for a dive-bombing run in an F-4*. And with that, my fear was gone. What was there to be afraid of? It was after all, only half as steep as a dive-bombing run in an F-4. This is what it was to be an Air Force fighter pilot's son.

I also remember going with my family to Cape Canaveral in the early 1980s to see my uncle's launch into space. When the rockets piggybacked to the space shuttle lit, the sound physically rumbled through me as if I was sitting on one of those massage chairs at a Brookstone store. I also remember thinking how inconvenient it was to be in the friends-and-family bleachers three miles away, because it was hard to see what was happening on the pad where the space shuttle was. It never occurred to me until years later that we were so far away because the engineers calculated that was the minimum safe distance for us in case something went wrong at liftoff.

This was my life as a boy. Fighter jets, Air Force bases, and space shuttle launches.

I guess I never thought much of it.

So, on Blatt's recommendation, I called my uncle and asked if he would fly down from the Bay Area and give a talk for me.

I explained what I wanted him to do and why I needed him to do it, and after the obligatory ribbing about the downward trajectory of my professional life (*from attorney to politician, what's next?*), I found he was genuinely excited about it. He came down a few weeks later.

My uncle told me he sometimes spoke to engineering and science classes at schools and universities, so when I found out he would be coming, I contacted the principal of our local middle school and asked if she'd like to have him speak with one of her science classes. She liked the idea, but she didn't want him to speak *just* to a science class.

I picked up my uncle at LAX airport on the afternoon of May 4, 2006, and after a quick lunch, I delivered him to the assembly room at Valley Middle School in Hermosa Beach.

Waiting for him in neat rows were the entire fifth, seventh, and eighth grades (the sixth grade was on a field trip that day, I think). When I saw the sea of young faces and the barely controlled commotion, I was a little worried. Sure, my uncle had been an Air Force test pilot, had flown spacecraft, and had even worked on joint missions with the Soviets . . . but how was he going to deal with a room filled with three hundred adolescents?

The astronaut had it handled. He brought slides of his launches and video he and other astronauts had shot in space with a handheld camera. Within seconds the students were mesmerized. They wanted to know what it was like sleeping in a weightless environment. *It's like sleeping on a cloud,* he said. The astronaut didn't miss a beat when one kid (there's always one) asked how they used the bathroom if there wasn't any gravity to flush a toilet. *Very carefully,* the astronaut said, and then explained the process involved a vacuum. The students were captivated by the idea of space, and the man standing before them who had been there. They loved hearing his stories, but I could tell that the old astronaut probably loved telling them more.

Afterwards, when I shared my previous trepidation with my uncle, he told me he had given that talk many times. Public relations, he said, was an important part of what astronauts did. Because the agency had been born during the Space Race with the Soviets in the early 1960s, NASA knew full well that there was a political and PR component to its continued viability. I'd never really considered that, but it made perfect sense. The American public needed to know we were putting a man into space, and that we were technologically superior to the Soviets. Some people know that Cosmonaut Yuri Gagarin was the first man to go into orbit, but every man, woman, and child on Earth knows that American Neil Armstrong was the first man on the moon. It was part of every astronaut's official duty to speak with the public about what they did. I had been worried for nothing. My uncle had had plenty of practice.

A few hours later, my uncle was talking to a roomful of my supporters at the art gallery. The people gathered that night were no less taken with his stories than the kids at the middle school had been—maybe more so, many of them having grown up during the Space Race. One resident brought with him an unopened pack of cigarettes that commemorated the Apollo-Soyuz mission, and presented them to my uncle as if he were returning an artifact to the proprietor of a museum. Another resident who had worked on some aspect of the space program and had met my uncle in the late 1960s wanted to shake his hand again. I had never been in an environment like this with my uncle. His accomplishments—and the public's fascination with NASA and the guys who had what Tom Wolfe famously called "The Right Stuff"—still inspired admiration and awe.

The papers picked up the story of my uncle's visit to the local school. My name, which I happened to share with a famous astronaut, was in all the papers that week. It was also fun to think about how many parents heard about an unusual use for a vacuum when they asked their kids what they learned in school that day.

To top it off, we raised a good amount of money at the art gallery event. The day was a success.

Apart from the expensive, newly yellow-tinted painting, that is.

⁓

It didn't take long to find the yellow-bottomed culprit. He was standing along the wall near the chafing dishes with a plate of hors d'oeuvres. The smeared, bright acrylic was visible on the seat of his black jeans. It was Alonzo, one of my earliest supporters. He was at my fundraiser that night because he wanted me to remember that he'd supported me when I needed him.

I walked up to Alonzo with the stern, cross-armed curator tailing me like she thought I might make a break for it.

Alonzo, I said, *your butt is yellow. And it looks like you've been rubbing it on paintings.*

The words took a moment to register. He first looked confused, as though his dog had walked into the kitchen at breakfast and asked for coffee. He understood all the words, but what he heard didn't make any sense.

Then his eyes got big. *Oh, my butt is yellow!*

The curator's glare must have confirmed the problem.

I must have leaned against it, he said, apologetically.

I don't know how Alonzo and the curator finally rectified the problem. He told me he would handle it, and I didn't ask further. It seemed crass to ask the guy for a $250 campaign contribution and then send him home with a very expensive art piece. But it was a very cool painting. I wonder if Alonzo has it hanging in his living room, the bottom fringe hidden behind the couch? I'm sure if anyone asked him, he would tell them it was a reminder of how expensive local politics can be.

SECRET No. 3
Know Thyself

What's a Nice Candidate Like You Doing in a Place Like This?

It was a standard-issue witness interview room: small, white, and windowless. There were three of us there, the two Hermosa Beach police officers and me. They were probably in their mid-thirties, and both were wearing their game faces.

One game face had a fresh black eye.

We were sitting at a hard plastic and metal table, the kind you would find in a local high school lunchroom. The officers were on one side and I sat across from them. Maybe twenty-four inches separated us. I don't think there was a steel loop on the table for manacles, and I didn't check to see if there was one on the floor. So far as I knew, I hadn't been charged with anything.

There was probably a video camera in the corner of the ceiling watching me, and in retrospect, I realize my interview was likely recorded so other officers could evaluate my performance. I am sure the *uh-oh* expression on my face upon entering the room was freeze-framed for posterity. Or perhaps the interview was beamed into another room via closed-circuit so officers could pass judgment in real time.

I had come to the station for this interview at the officers' invitation, and when they met me in the lobby I don't recall a

Secret No. 3 – Know Thyself

handshake or even an exchange of the most basic pleasantries. There was a curt introduction, and then straight here to the interview room.

So, I said to the officer with the purple mouse under his eye, *I hope you didn't get that from the previous interview.* I smiled. No need for all the seriousness; this was only an informal interview, right?

Crickets. Captain Kirk just told a knock-knock joke to Mister Spock.

I got this last night, the officer said without any acknowledgement of my attempt to lighten the uncomfortable situation. *We had to subdue a suspect.*

I tried my best to display the appropriate level of masculine concern for another man who had been injured in the line of duty. The puffy purple evidence on his face of whatever had gone down the night before looked less like *subdue* and a lot more like *fight* to me. If nothing else, I was determined not to do anything that would get me *subdued*. The camera watching me from the corner of the room had an off switch.

This wasn't an interview you'd conduct with a prospective employee. Those interviews took place at coffee shops, or at a restaurant over lunch. Whatever this was, it carried with it a subtle yet palpable threat.

The small, closed, windowless room in the basement and what the officers did once we got there vaguely reminded me of the resistance training I'd received in the military.

The Air Force called it resistance training, but that was euphemistic military-speak; it was the training we got to prepare us should we ever become prisoners of war. The interrogations I'd been subjected to at a mock POW camp in the woods outside of Colorado Springs bore more than a passing resemblance to what I was going through in this basement in the Hermosa Beach police department. Both occurred in windowless rooms at a simple table with people trying to impress upon me that *they* were in control of the situation. The main difference was that the guys interrogating me during my Air Force training were rugged sergeants (ominously and appropriately nicknamed *snake eaters*) in Russian-style uniforms doing their best Boris Badenov accents.

There is an old saying that even a dog knows the difference between being tripped over and being kicked. A person being interviewed knows the difference between an interview and an interrogation. I'd been through both, and this was an interrogation. With their humorless demeanors and stern faces, these two cops were trying their best to approximate what the Air Force sergeants had done by merely walking into the room: set the tone and establish that they were in charge. This stage production in the windowless basement room had another goal as well—the officers wanted to intimidate me.

What had I done to find myself seated at a table in a witness interrogation room with these two Hermosa Beach police officers?

I was running for City Council.

This was my candidate interview with two representatives from the police union. Presumably, all they knew about me at that point was that I was a fiscally conservative Republican. It was my first interaction with them; I had never met the two officers before. In fact, this was the first interaction I'd ever had with the Hermosa Beach police.

Where Do You Come From?

Nobody really likes strangers, at least not at first. The impulse to sort people into the ones we know and the ones we don't know is a survival instinct that has worked for our species for millennia. It's a basic human reaction to be wary of outsiders, and playing to that instinct works, which is why that tactic is so often used in politics.

When I first ran for city council, the comment I kept hearing was that I "came out of nowhere." I hadn't grown up in Hermosa Beach, didn't go to the local schools, didn't own a business here, and wasn't related to long-term Hermosa residents. (I served with one councilman who was fond of telling constituents that he'd lived in Hermosa Beach so long he *remembered when they put the beach in*.) But that didn't mean I didn't love my new home. I did. I wanted to contribute to the community, so I settled in and reached out.

No matter how new you are to a town—or how disconnected you might feel—it is always possible to create the ties to the community that will support your run for office. There are steps you can take to sow those seeds.

The simplest approach is to get involved in something. It doesn't matter what you choose; go to a Rotary, women's club, or historical society meeting. There are dozens of ways to integrate yourself into the fabric of your community. In Hermosa Beach, for example, fundraising for the local schools is a constant, year-long process, which means there is always an opportunity to participate. Youth sports events are another option. Here in Hermosa Beach, for instance, there's a subculture of Little League dads always repairing fields and working on projects to improve the Little League park. The chances to pitch in and contribute are all around, and most of the things you'll get involved in are actually fun, too. Build up your community, and they'll build up their trust in you.

While you're strengthening your ties to the community, get to work on your message. It's one of the most important things you'll do for your campaign. You may not win with a good message, but you'll almost certainly lose with a bad one. Pick something simple and clear that will resonate with the electorate.

Where Are You Going?

Once you have your message defined, you'll have an opportunity to write out a candidate statement. The candidate statement is typically limited to a few hundred words that tell voters what you think is most important for them to know about your candidacy.

Some candidates choose not to write this, or they aren't organized enough to fully articulate their message by the time the sample ballot goes to print. But the smart ones have worked out their message long in advance. The sample ballot (and your candidate statement) reach more people than you could ever hope to talk to—every registered voter in your district—so the message written in it may end up being the only thing many voters know about you. To get a good idea of how to effectively write a candidate statement, look at the statements written by experienced, incumbent candidates. There's no guarantee their statements are the reason they won, but they're clearly doing something right.

Don't overlook advertising. The 1960 presidential campaign saw Nixon and Kennedy both reach out to professional ad men, using the newfangled medium of television to accomplish the old-school political goal of selling themselves to the public, just like breakfast cereal and Buicks. The indelible mark television has left on campaign marketing can still be seen in the way campaigns define their candidates: Catch phrases, flashy slogans, and anything that gets the candidate's persona across quickly have become much more important than they once were. Television made identifying a candidate to the public much easier, and it made responding to the accusations of other candidates much simpler.

As a newcomer to politics, you may be saying to yourself, *But I don't have the kind of budget you need to run a TV spot!* And you'd be right. Turning directly to an advertising agency right off the bat skips several important steps, vacuums up your budget, and is undoubtedly a fool's path. Look for a local consultant first. Consultants can act as mid-level ad people who can help you define who you are, what you want to accomplish, and what you want people to know about you. During my first campaign, for instance, my opponent was perceived to be an angry old man, fitting right in with the *Get off my lawn!* stereotype, so the consultant we hired branded me as a young, clean-cut former military man—energetic and trustworthy.

Getting your message out through traditional means has its place, but you cannot ignore social media. Join all the important social media platforms (Facebook, Twitter, Instagram, LinkedIn, etc.) and be busy on them. Some campaigns hire college students or have young volunteers monitor the candidate's various social media accounts. At a minimum, make sure your hard work, community involvement, and endorsements get posted to your accounts. A voter who finds his way to your Facebook page should see exactly how busy you are, and what you're doing to better serve their needs. People need to see reason after reason why they should vote for you.

Social media is also on occasion a good way to keep up with what your opponents are doing. Did they attend an event you didn't know about? Are they doing something you intended to do? This kind of information is becoming increasingly available and thus increasingly important. Like sample ballots, social media frames you in a way that reaches people you may never speak to.

Remember, the crucial part of your message isn't repeating who you are or what you've done. The people in your district may be impressed with your accolades and past accomplishments, but what they really want to know is what you plan do for the community! Be sure to tell them.

The most important thing is to explain to the voter, over and over again, as clearly as possible, why you would be a better voice for their district than your opponents. You do this every time you speak, every time you work to build up your community, every time you stand up for what you believe in. It is the cumulative effect of clearly articulating your identity, your history, your hopes for your community, and the concrete steps you're going to take to bring those hopes into reality. Every community needs a strong voice to speak for it. Your task as a candidate is to convince voters that you are that voice.

Where Are You Vulnerable?

The art of campaigning rests on showcasing why you are the best choice for the district. This is no secret. Your opponent will try to expose your weaknesses just as hard as you'll work to expose theirs. Don't let them do it. Know your issues from back

Secret No. 3 – Know Thyself

to front, and keep an eye on your own vulnerabilities. Never say anything you aren't certain of, or make assumptions about an issue that you haven't examined in depth. Someone else will take advantage of your uncertainty and use it to make you look foolish. Stick tightly to your message.

There's a lot to be said about debates, but the oldest advice is still probably the most important: Preparation is essential. Find videos online of the last election's debates. With an election every two years, the issues probably haven't changed too much. Take particular note of the questions that are asked.

Practice is also important. Sit down and write out the questions you think will come up and the issues you'll focus on, and then practice answering those questions and bringing up those points with another person. It is especially important to practice your opening, because if you get off to a good start, the rest will flow better. Most people don't particularly like public speaking, and even if they do, practice is still essential to a smooth performance.

Remember that anyone can host a debate or a candidate forum, so be discerning about which ones you attend. Stick with the traditional ones, and go to every single one of them.

Similarly, try to attend as many clubs and civic meetings as you can find. You don't have to be there long—you can show up for ten minutes, shake some hands, and then leave—but showing that you care enough about the community to make an appearance can go a long way. Be sure you deliver a canned minute of your message before you go.

The key takeaway is that the more times you can present yourself and your message, the more likely it is that people will recognize your name and remember it when they head to the polls.

Will You Endorse Me?

The public employee unions are the modern-day Praetorian Guard of California politics. Like their Roman forebears, California's union Praetorians evolved from an organization that merely protected their political masters into a political force that ruled in their own right by using their financial and political muscle to select their own bosses.[3] The police and firefighters' unions are typically at the vanguard of this effort at the local level, but public unions are enmeshed in electoral politics at every level from the White House to the local school board.

At the state and national level public unions tend to select Democrats as their bosses, but in local nonpartisan races they are less discriminating. A Republican city councilman who will reliably vote to increase union members' salaries, pensions, and benefits is just as good as a Democratic one. In exchange, compliant politicians receive union money and support at election time. This arrangement would end quickly if the unions were unable to win elections. But they do, and there are three reasons for this:

First, at the local level the unions almost always have more resources than their opponents do. They have money to spend and a ready-made pool of people willing to work on campaigns. Second, the public trusts its police and firefighters, and the

---

[3] Like California's public employee unions, the Roman praetorians weren't above using their power for personal gain. For example, in A.D. 193 the praetorians murdered the emperor Pertinax and then auctioned the right to succeed him to the highest bidder.

Secret No. 3 – Know Thyself

police and firefighters trade on this this trust. Third, and most important, the unions have the political will and corresponding readiness to do the things, both legitimate and illegitimate, that are necessary to win elections.

Wait a minute, rewind. The unions do unprincipled and unscrupulous things to win elections? Sometimes, yes. Sure, lots of people on both sides of the aisle do. But the public safety unions' willingness to do what is necessary to win an election can take a dark turn. The police unions, at their worst, intimidate, threaten, and harass. As I came to learn, the Hermosa Beach police union had no compunction about doing whatever it deemed necessary to a political rival who threatened the *status quo*.

I once had a date tell me Hermosa cops stopped her on the Strand, a popular pedestrian walkway that runs the length of our beach. *For what?* I asked. She said the officers had seen the two of us together a few nights before and wanted to warn her about the company she kept.

Be careful, they told her, *the mayor is trouble.*

This was an egregious and patently illegal abuse of their authority. But the message needed to be sent—to her, for sure, but to me too. The police wanted me to know they were watching.

I guess I should be relieved I didn't live in Stockton. Forced into bankruptcy by the city's onerous union contracts, Stockton had to cut costs by reducing its pension obligations. The police union communicated its displeasure with this idea by purchasing the home next door to the city manager, who was the person at city hall ultimately responsible for the cutbacks. The police

Nine Secrets for Getting Elected

union said it was just looking to diversify its portfolio, and it was probably just a coincidence that the purchase of that investment property occurred on the same day labor negotiations broke down. It was also likely just an unfortunate happenstance that this investment required considerable remodeling and landscaping. At all hours, and especially during the Stockton city manager's grandson's birthday party. As I soon found out, in Stockton, as in Hermosa Beach, as in everywhere else in California, nothing was off-limits.

This is truly despicable stuff, especially because the people doing it are the same people the public trusts to protect our families and keep our homes safe. So why does it happen? My theory is that police unions view their political opponents through the same crime-fighting lens with which police tend view the rest of the world. The problem is that tactics and methods that are appropriate to use against gangsters and criminals on the street are wholly inappropriate to use against someone who merely holds a different political viewpoint.

⁐

Every community has a core group of people who influence everyone else, which means that an endorsement from any of these people can carry some significant weight. Getting someone known and respected to publicly support you eases the voters' minds. Look to people like the Chamber of Commerce, the PTA, or any city council members not currently in competition with you. Ask early for their endorsements, and when you get them (in writing), make sure that everyone else knows you've

Secret No. 3 – Know Thyself

gotten them. An endorsement is no good to you if only you know about it.

The asking itself can be pretty personal. It's a bit like asking someone to prom—sometimes complete with sweaty hands and goose bumps (okay, maybe that was just *my* prom). As soon as you decide to run, make these phone calls—because if you're not first, someone else will be—and make a solid case for why you deserve their endorsement. You want them to like you enough to endorse you, or at a minimum make it hard for them to endorse one of your opponents.

Sometimes you can lock in an endorsement by pledging to support them the next time they have to run, but it's not always that simple. The essential metric will always be this: Do you have something they need? If you can make their job easier, they'll be better disposed towards working with you.

It's not unheard of for influencers to endorse multiple people for the sake of covering their bases, so it's your job to give them a good reason to not do that. That said, while dual endorsements may seem like a loss, they actually mean that the endorsement your opponent won has been defanged, which goes in your win column. The same goes for someone who wants to continue working with you but is concerned that endorsing you might anger their constituency. If they agree to endorse no one, you've successfully prevented your opponent from winning that endorsement.

Public employee unions are usually the first stop for a candidate looking for endorsements, and not for the reason you think. There's a perception that winning the endorsement of the police officers' union or the firefighters' means that the candidate is running on a law and order platform, or that the endorsement of public unions at all is limited to Democrats. Not so.

Remember, like almost everything in public life, *it's about money*.

With their endorsement, the unions are looking to establish relationships that will benefit them when it comes time for the city council to discuss their members' pay and benefits.[4]

This isn't unusual.

You may have decided to run with the purest of intentions—*I want to serve the people's interests!*—but every community has groups that profit from their influence in city hall. These are people who look at your hopeful, earnest campaign and see a way to pay their mortgage or send their kids to college or buy a vacation home on Lake Havasu. They take it very seriously.

Which isn't to say that you should avoid their endorsements. After all, you're not just getting their stature in the community. Alongside the expectations of backscratching come potentially thousands of dollars in campaign contributions, as well as union-paid campaign workers who will walk their precincts for you, door-to-door. It can have a huge effect. One of my early competitors, Cliff Clouseau, started his campaign with practically nothing, but received the endorsement of the police officers' union to the tune of $15,000. And it was enough to put him over the top on Election Day.

---

[4] A popular Orange County political blog reported that in one predominantly Latino, overwhelmingly Democratic city, the police union's endorsement and the hundreds of thousands of dollars that came with it were contingent on a promise from the candidate that he or she would vote to fire the city's current police chief and city manager if he or she won the election.

Think hard about what that might mean to your campaign before moving one way or another with union endorsements. And think hard about how a long-term relationship with these unions could affect the decisions you make as an elected official.

Making Enemies

When Costa Mesa Mayor Jim Righeimer's wife told him a cop was at the front door, he knew something was wrong. Officers would sometimes come to his home if there was an emergency, but Righeimer had just been with Costa Mesa's police chief a few hours prior at a community event. If something were going on he would have heard about it.

The officer asked Righeimer to step outside. *This is not good,* he thought. By this time, Righeimer's three young daughters had come to the door to see what the commotion was with their father and the policeman at the door. Wishing to avoid any sort of confrontation, and trying to keep his girls from being afraid of whatever was about to happen, Righeimer stepped out of his home onto his patio.

His wife and three daughters, 6, 8, and 10, were right there with him, watching.

The officer told the mayor that someone had called 911 to report that he had been driving under the influence. Righeimer had just driven home from Skosh Monahan's, a local pub owned by Righeimer's city council colleague Gary Monahan, but the mayor hadn't consumed any alcohol there. Righeimer had had two sodas, and later produced the receipt from the bar to prove it. The officer nevertheless conducted a field sobriety test on the mayor's front porch, in front of his frightened wife and three now-teary little girls.

Something was definitely off, but it was not unexpected. Righeimer had locked horns with Costa Mesa's public employee unions over their salaries, pensions, and benefits, and knew he was in their crosshairs. A fiscal conservative and businessman himself, Righeimer was unapologetically vocal about his efforts to bring the city's labor costs under control. He was probably the most vocal critic of public employee unions in Orange County, and perhaps in all of Southern California.

Righeimer passed his sobriety test.

The next day he went to the press with what happened.

It was a set-up, he said.

When the 911 call that reported him driving erratically after leaving Skosh Monahan's became public, it was clear that the mayor's suspicions were correct.

The man who had made the 911 call was a former Riverside police officer who worked as a private investigator for the law firm that represented the Costa Mesa police union. The private investigator told the police dispatcher Righeimer had stumbled out of the bar and swerved all the way home.

Why was the investigator at the bar? He was there surveilling the mayor because Costa Mesa's unions needed to smear him and his credibility. Righeimer was too vocal and had been much too effective in reeling in the costs associated with the benefits the city paid its employees, and even a trace of alcohol on his breath would have been enough to undermine him politically. A DUI arrest would create a firestorm of scrutiny that would effectively drown out anything else Mayor Righeimer did. Righeimer's arrest would be a rallying point for his opponents and might cost him the next election. That's why the private investigator was following him. He had just seen Righeimer consume two drinks and knew he would hit the jackpot if the mayor got pulled over with any alcohol in his system.

The private investigator called 911 to report the mayor's alleged drunk driving, followed him all the way home, and parked his car just up the street to watch the Costa Mesa police officer conduct a sobriety test on Righeimer's front porch.

As a first-time candidate, your job is to be as inclusive as possible, partly to seem like less of a threat, and partly because people are looking to newbie politicians for hope: everyone wants to think of their shiny, new city councilman as a modern Mr. Smith. All of which means that the appearance of your integrity is paramount, so avoid personal mudslinging. That said, by all means, go after your opponent's terrible ideas. Just refrain from pointing out that he's had a personal bankruptcy and is late on his child-support payments. Other people will invariably bring these things up without you having to say a word.

Wherever there is an active, militant police officers' or firefighters' union there is usually a lawyer somewhere just off-stage, feeding its leadership their lines. In Hermosa Beach, the police union's leadership has a cozy relationship with a local attorney who might be viewed less as a traditional legal counselor and more as the union's *consigliere*. He was more Tom Hagen than Oscar Goodman.

It is no surprise that a review of lawsuits filed by Hermosa Beach police against the city is a who's who of the union leadership. The *consigliere* obtained a promotion for the current police union president through litigation. In other cases the *consigliere* defended his union flock when they were guilty of misconduct. In 1998, two officers kept their jobs when they were caught by US customs agents attempting to smuggle steroids across the border from Tijuana. In another instance, the department's use-of-force instructor avoided any consequential discipline after he punched out a civilian at a local karaoke bar. The civilian earned the free, unarmed combat demonstration because he was unimpressed with the instructor's rendition of Marvin Gaye's "Sexual Healing."

Sadly, this type of symbiotic relationship between a union and a particular lawyer or law firm is typical. Costa Mesa's police union was represented by the law firm that literally wrote the book on representing officers—Lackie, Dammeier & McGill. The name partner at that firm, Dieter Dammeier, was the *capo di tutti capi* of the police union *consiglieri*.

Dammeier's firm had a reputation for hardball tactics, and had grown a considerable practice because of it. "The reason we represent most of the [police unions] in LA, Orange, Riverside, and San Bernardino counties is because police officers like and on occasion require aggressive representation," Dammeier said in an interview. Many of the lawyers were former police officers themselves. "Former Cops Defending Current Ones," the

Secret No. 3 – Know Thyself

firm's website boasted. At the height of its influence, the firm represented 120 police unions and 18 of the 39 police unions in Orange County.

The Dammeier firm was brash about its success. Its website featured testimonials from police union clients who were thrilled with the firm's ability to bring city councils to their knees during labor negotiations. Dammeier and his law firm were so brazen about their strong-arm successes that they published a how-to guide for pressuring and intimidating city councils during labor negotiations. They called this tutorial *The Playbook*.

Comparing its recommendations to the use-of-force guidelines police follow before drawing a gun or using their Tasers on a suspect, *The Playbook* likewise suggested that unions "start with simple verbal commands." If things did not progress to their liking, "jump to a higher level, based on the circumstances." *The Playbook* did not contain talking points designed to win the public debate about pensions and salaries; it was a blueprint for strong-arm coercion.

What were the actual plays in *The Playbook*? It told officers to storm city councils and publicly chastise elected officials about their lack of concern for public safety. It recommended that officers appear at civic events such as Christmas tree lightings and make the public aware that the police union was upset about this lack of concern for public safety. *The Playbook* recommended starting websites to attack the city. "'**GardenGroveSucks.com**' was a big hit," *The Playbook* said.

The book also recommended that police unions take advantage of high profile crimes. Each one "should result in the association's uproar" at the city council "for not having enough officers on the street, which could have [prevented] the incident." During elections, *The Playbook* recommended campaigning against union-unfriendly council members for their "lack of concern for public safety." Most directly, *The Playbook* said to focus energy on one city official at a time. "Focus on a city manager, councilperson, mayor, or police chief, and keep the pressure up until that person assures you [of] his loyalty, and then move to the next victim."

Sheep's Clothing

The police and firefighters get their members more money because they have an advantage no one else in politics does—the public trusts them. Most people like their local police, particularly in smaller towns, and people almost universally love their firefighters. We have great faith in these groups, as we should.

Try to remember the last time you were actually face-to-face with a firefighter. Unless you were in grave danger or your house was on fire, you probably can't. Remember 9/11? Photographs of soot-faced NYFD officers standing on the rubble? That's what most people think about when they think about firefighters. And they should. Those guys are brave and willing to do things most people are not.

But unions are different. They don't exist to serve or protect the public. To the contrary, unions exist exclusively for the benefit of themselves and their members. There is no way for the public to discern where legitimate public safety activities end and political union activity begins, and the police and firefighter unions do everything they can to blur that line.

The Costa Mesa police union fired Dammeier and his firm moments before Righeimer held a press conference to talk about what Dammeier and his private investigator had done. But firing the law firm that published *The Playbook* didn't keep the story from getting worse.

It turned out the private investigator wasn't just in the bar to follow Righeimer home. No, he was there with a woman he'd hired. She was what Ian Fleming might have referred to in one of his novels as a honeypot: The theory goes that her job was to flirt with Costa Mesa Councilman Gary Monahan, the owner of the bar, and put him in a compromising position that Dammeier could then exploit in the ongoing labor negotiations. The city councilman avoided the trap.

Despicable as this plot was, it is even more troubling on another level. What did Dammeier intend to do with whatever compromising information he obtained from his busty trap, had he gotten something useful? Were they going to run an ad in the local paper with a photograph of the woman and Monahan and a *New York Daily News*–style headline? Were they going to send a piece of mail to the public proclaiming that Monahan had stepped outside his marriage? Of course not. I'm sure the people who did it thought they were merely gaining leverage over a political opponent for use privately, quietly, in a one-on-one phone call. But others, particularly prosecutors and DAs might call this type of leverage by its proper legal name—extortion.

The story gets worse. When the FBI raided Dammeier's law offices in the wake of this scandal, they discovered the firm had a spreadsheet containing a list of all the places the third conservative Costa Mesa city councilman, Steve Mensinger, had been.

How did Dammeier's firm get that information? It was too exact—complete with latitude and longitude—to have been the product of a conventional tail. What was it?

GPS. Someone had attached a GPS tracker to Mensinger's truck while it sat in his driveway.

Dammeier's firm eventually admitted what it had done. *So what,* they asked, *if the law firm tracked the councilman's truck as it drove on public streets? It was visible to any member of the public anyway—where's the harm?*

⁓

At some point, police and firefighters decided to call themselves "associations," eschewing the loaded term *union* and all that it implies. So instead of being the police officer's union, they're the much more benign and helpful-sounding Police Officers' Association (POA). Like the National Basketball Association, the Association of Realtors, or the Parent-Teacher Association. Same idea. Because everyone can name an association that does something good. It is hard to find people who can say the same thing about a union, however, unless you're in one.

These associations are typically organized as nonprofits and do the all-American things you think of when you think about police and firefighters. For example, in Hermosa Beach, the Firefighters' Association holds a pancake breakfast at the station house. The firefighters move the ladder-truck and ambulances out of the port and put in grills and removable tables. There's a silent auction of memorabilia donated by local celebrities— for example, a hockey stick signed by Los Angeles Kings, or a

Secret No. 3 – Know Thyself

volleyball signed by a local Olympian, may sit on a table with a clipboard bearing bids. Children slide down the freshly polished brass pole that connects the second-story sleeping quarters with the bay. For the rest of the day you can spot kids with little red firefighter hats and HBFD stickers all over town. These functions are similar to activities conducted by dyed-in-the-wool community service groups, like the Kiwanis Club or the local historical society. And if the associations' activities stopped with hosting pancake breakfasts and Little League, the world would be a better place. Unfortunately, as Mayor Righeimer and Stockton's city manager will attest, they don't.

⁓

The police and firefighters' unions also have political arms that are separate from their nonprofit, community outreach sides. Federal tax and state campaign finance laws mandate that political activity be separated from everything else, although it is nearly impossible for the public to separate the two. The nonprofit associations can't raise or spend money for political activities, so the unions form political action committees, or PACs to do that. The PACs are the pointy end of the unions' political spear.

Until now, you've probably never heard of your local police or firefighters' PAC. The police and firefighters know "PAC" sounds too political and too clever, so they give their political organizations euphonious names like Firefighters for Better Government or Police Protective League. The circumlocution masks the activity. The police and firefighters' PACs exist to raise, donate, and spend money during political campaigns. They run ads supporting candidates they like and hit pieces against candidates they don't.

The police and firefighters' unions know exactly what their strengths are and how to play to them. Their message is always very clear—support our candidate and vote for what we want, and you, your children, and your home will be safe. Vote for the other candidate, or against what the unions want, and your family, home, and community will be at risk.

For example, at the peak of the battle during Stockton's bankruptcy, the police union paid for billboards at the city's entrance welcoming visitors to "the second most dangerous city in California," and warning that "due to cuts in the budget, we can no longer guarantee your safety." The city manager's phone number was listed at the bottom of the signs.[5] The unions have one pitch, and like a Mariano Rivera fastball, it's still hard to deal with even though you know it's coming.

Sound extreme? Hardly. During my last budget negotiation, the Hermosa Beach police and firefighters' unions staged a public relations campaign designed to frighten the public. The unions were not getting satisfaction from the city council, so they decided to go straight to the residents. The public would pressure the city council members to accede to the unions' demands for raises.

Their tactics came straight from *The Playbook*.

Taking Your District's Temperature

The economic downturn in 2007–08 hit municipalities just as

---

5 Alyssia Finley, "To Serve and Protect—Police Pensions," Wall Street Journal (January 11, 2013).

Secret No. 3 – Know Thyself

hard as it hit everyone else. Many cities were forced to lay off employees, and a number of nearby cities imposed furloughs. Hermosa Beach didn't lay anyone off or impose furloughs, but the arithmetic was clear: we didn't have the money to give pay increases. The city council pared the payroll by giving golden handshakes to older employees and hired only mission-critical replacements. This kept us out of the fiscal quicksand that was swallowing cities all around us. This was not the situation to which the unions had grown accustomed, particularly from their allies on the city council.

So the Hermosa Beach police union did what *The Playbook* suggested. They unilaterally decreed that California was in full recovery and that Hermosa Beach's municipal coffers were full. They wanted the public to think there was money for them, and they wanted what they had always gotten: more.

The fright offensive against the public started with a push poll. A push poll is a method of implanting information with voters under the guise of conducting a survey. For example, the police union's political consultants (yes, of course they have them) called the city's high-propensity voters and asked if they would support a 27 percent cut to the police department. (*No! Of course not!*) They asked the residents if they would feel better or worse about those cuts knowing that the city council had increased its own budget by 10 percent during that same period. (*What? Those greedy bastards!*) They wanted to know if the public would support cuts to the fire department's budget if those cuts meant their response to an emergency would be 10 percent slower. (*I'm calling those City Council members as soon as we hang up!*)

The Hermosa unions then sent out slick mailers to every resident with the "statistics" they'd gathered during the push poll. The banner across the top of one mail piece said, "In a recent poll, 93 percent of you TRUSTED Police and Fire vs. 7 percent for city council." Having been spoon-fed deceptive questions larded with erroneous statistics, I'm surprised the city council got even 7 percent. Or maybe it was like the old Soviet elections, in which the Communist Party would announce their victory with 95 percent of the vote. I always wondered who was brave enough to be in the remaining 5 percent, or if that sliver of dissent was only included to lend credibility to the overall result. A 100 percent rate was not believable, but 93 percent? Maybe. Even in a worker's paradise like Cuba or the Soviet Union, there will always be a few people who don't know what's good for them.

The union also took its fright campaign to the press. The president of the firefighters' union told the local paper, "For those of us committed to risking our lives to save others, it seems that [the] city council has lost sight of its number-one priority, which is to protect the community." The mail the police union sent to the trusting public echoed this line: "We continue to be committed to PROTECTING YOU AND YOUR FAMILY. We are well-trained professionals who have made long-term commitments to serving your community, TO RISKING OUR LIVES TO SAVE YOURS." The unions are very disciplined about staying on their message.

The Hermosa Beach police and firefighters also showed up to city council meetings, always in uniform (remember, council meetings are televised), to emphasize their commitment to the community. Radios on their belts crackling with traffic, the police and firefighters' union reps never missed the opportunity to express their disappointment in public, just as *The Playbook* recommended. They stood before the city council and asked with an air of disbelief how elected officials could vote for a budget that would make their city's residents less safe.

Hermosa Beach's residents predictably responded to the fear mongering. As soon as the push poll started, I received phone calls.

But the numbers weren't accurate. They were half-truths and outright misrepresentations designed to press the city council into increasing their pay and benefits. The police union never cited any basis for their allegation that a 27 percent cut was on the negotiation table. It certainly wasn't part of the city's bargaining position. If the police union wanted the city council to buy each of its members a $1 lottery ticket and the city council refused, the unions would send out mailers and make phone calls telling the public "City Council Missed Opportunity at Millions in New Funding for Public Safety."

The police union was feeding the public abject, contemptible bunk.

⤻

Depending on your budget, polling is worth the investment. Not on yourself—save that kind of research for later in the campaign—but on issues that are important to the voter. If you're running on a platform of say, reforming zoning laws and business tax licenses, you'll want to know how the community feels about those issues. You'll want to know what things the voters are most concerned about so you can frame your issues in a way that responds to those concerns. Eventually, sure, you'll talk to enough people and get a solid bead on their feelings, but pushing a poll early on can give you a jump on the things that would otherwise take a while to learn.

If polling is outside your budget, you should know that hiring your own polling company isn't the only way to go. You can pick up a lot of information simply by observing the other political operations around you. Lots of groups do their own polling. Special interest groups are usually in favor of the incumbent, so if you see them happy over their polling numbers, be concerned. There's also simply calling in favors. Corporations, unions, and anyone with the interest and the money to do their own polling might be willing to give you a heads-up on how well your candidacy is progressing.

༄

What if the US military used the same campaign tactics the public safety unions do and tried to cash in on the public's trust? Imagine this commercial running during the next federal election cycle:

Setting: A dry, dusty, mountainous road in a desolate place that resembles Afghanistan or Northern Iraq.

Scene: A column of dusty infantrymen in full kit, patrolling. Each of the soldiers carries his rifle at the ready.

[Camera approaches the column from the opposite direction, slows to focus on the first soldier.]

Secret No. 3 – Know Thyself

Speaking Soldier #1: *We've been tracking a Taliban leader who was part of 9/11. Intel says he's up here training ISIS jihadists for another attack on America. We're going to stop them.*

[Camera moves to next soldier in the column.]

Speaking Soldier #2: *ISIS is a tough, determined enemy, and we need better equipment to fight them. But Congressman* [insert name of targeted congressman here] *voted against giving us the things we need.*

[Camera moves to next soldier in the column.]

Speaking Soldier #3: *Yeah, I heard* [insert name of targeted congressman here] *voted to spend tax dollars for a new cart path at his local golf course instead of buying us better body armor.*

Speaking Soldier #4: *But* [insert favored candidate name here] *understands what it means to take a stand and fight. He's one of us. Vote for* [insert favored candidate name here] *and make sure we have what we need to protect your family, your children, and America from attack.*

[Distant sound of gunfire. Soldiers shout and start to move purposefully out of frame. Fade black. Red, white, and blue banner with *Vote for* [insert candidate name here] appears on screen. Announcer says, *This ad was approved by the Association to Protect Our Military Heroes.*]

Thankfully, this sort of election commercial hasn't happened (yet), and if it did, the outcry from the liberal left would be deafening. They would no doubt remind us all that it is against the Uniform Code of Military Justice (UCMJ) for military personnel to take part in partisan political activities. Historians would appear on CNN and CNBC to sound the constitutional alarm. They would tell the public that the Founding Fathers knew this was a path to disaster and remind us that military men from George Washington forward have been conspicuously absent from politics and elections. So strict are these restrictions that it is a crime for a military officer to even speak "contemptuous words" against the president. Remember General Stanley McChrystal? His distinguished thirty-four-year career in the Army was instantaneously extinguished after a few offhand comments appeared in *Rolling Stone*.

Now imagine if the same standards applied to the unions' leadership in local and state politics.

Or, alternatively, what if military personnel conducted interviews of congressional candidates, as the police union did with me? Or showed up at their homes? Or used intelligence services to attach GPS transponders to opposition leaders' cars to track their movements? Or did any of the things that public employee unions do in California?

This type of activity would be a direct threat to the foundation of our system of government. And yet we have surrendered our state to public employee unions who do exactly these things.

Keep Your Nose Out of My Rice Bowl

I didn't get the police union endorsement in the 2005 election cycle, and that was the last time I interviewed with any of the city's public unions. When I ran for reelection in 2009, I wrote a letter to the editor of one of the local weeklies and issued a press release stating that I would neither seek nor accept the endorsement of any public employee union during my campaign. I said it was a conflict of interest for elected officials to accept endorsements and money from the unions and then be expected to negotiate salary and benefit packages with those same groups while in office. I encouraged other candidates to take the same pledge. None of the other candidates did.

Despite the unions' best efforts to scuttle my campaign, I won reelection in 2009. But I had run up my colors for everyone to see, and the unions didn't like it.

As soon as I took office I stated my unequivocal intention to rein in pensions and salaries, and in doing so I became a confirmed Enemy of the Union State. The president of the police union went so far as to submit his own letter to the editor informing the public that I *had* in fact sought his union's endorsement, but that I did not receive it because the police union could not support someone who did not support public safety.

This was grade A horse manure.

This was a struggle for power in pursuit of money, and my vocal opposition was keeping the police union from acquiring more of both.

⌒

On Monday, August 30, 2010, a recently retired former president of the Hermosa Beach Firefighters Association lodged a complaint with the Los Angeles County District Attorney's Office alleging that I was not a resident of Hermosa Beach. The recently retired union president said the police and firefighters were convinced I was living at an address in nearby Redondo Beach.

If it was true I did not live in my district, this was a felony.

The evidence for the allegation was that the police officers who delivered official mail to my apartment never saw me at home, and I never answered the door when they came. The former union president said his colleagues in the department never saw lights on in my apartment when they returned to the station after calls at night. I guess I should have been comforted to know that the firefighters drove past my home so often, and that the police kept such close tabs on my apartment. Yet somehow, after reading the former union president's e-mail to the Los Angeles District Attorney, I didn't feel any safer.

The unions' concern about where my head hit the pillow at night and the concomitant surveillance of my home were aimed at one thing and one thing alone—invalidating my recent votes concerning their pensions and salaries.

The former union president said as much in his e-mail. If I was not a Hermosa Beach resident, "every opinion expressed and every vote cast by Mr. Bobko that was harmful to wages and benefits of city employees would warrant a legal remedy," he wrote.

According to this union man's e-mail, my voting record wasn't the only harmful thing; my political opinions were harmful, too.

If true, one legal remedy for my crime would be to revisit and invalidate each of the votes I'd cast concerning the unions' pensions and salaries. The other remedy, and the one that probably danced like a sugarplum in the union leaders' heads, would be to prove my guilt and have me arrested.

The timing of the e-mail wasn't a coincidence. The city council had recently completed the last round of contentious labor negotiations a few weeks earlier and implemented a cost-saving measure that incensed the unions. They were so angry about what we'd done that they sued to prevent the change from going into effect.

Word spread like wildfire that I supposedly lived in Redondo Beach and not Hermosa Beach. Reporters called to ask what I thought about the former union president's allegations. I told reporters I had made a compelling case for the cost-saving measures the city council had implemented, and this was proof they didn't have a substantive answer. It was a classic *ad hominem*, I said. Attack the person when you can't attack the argument.

I also invited the reporters to my home, and one reporter for a local online newspaper took me up on the offer. This reporter sat with me for an hour or so, and we talked about the recent pension and salary battles at city hall. She examined my bookshelves, looked at the address printed on the magazines on my coffee table, and asked about the family photographs hung on my walls.

Then she did something surprising—she went to the refrigerator and checked the expiration date on my carton of milk.

A day or so later another reporter came by my home and did the same thing.

They must teach reporters in journalism school to examine the expiration date on milk. But it makes sense; nobody would put a carton of perishable milk in a place where they didn't stay.

After their visits, all the reporters came to the same conclusion: the little apartment on the hill overlooking the beach was where I actually lived. (The Redondo Beach address was my youngest brother's place, where I'd stayed for a few months when I first moved to California.)

On September 3, 2010, I learned that the DA's office had opened an investigation into my residency. They never contacted me directly, and I was only aware of their activity from what I read in the papers—quotes like, *In the event of any breach of trust, the Public Integrity Division will investigate, and if appropriate, prosecute criminal misconduct by any elected or appointed official.* Even though I was completely in the clear, reading those words in print and realizing I was the target of a criminal investigation was unsettling. In retrospect, this was just a continuation of my first experience with the two cops in a small, windowless room in the basement at the police department.

The most unsettling aspect of this incident was the realization that members of the Hermosa Beach Police Department had been following me. I made no secret of my comings and goings and never thought I needed to. This wasn't East Germany, and the Hermosa Beach Police weren't the *Stasi*.

Were they?

⁓

In December of that year I learned from Jimmy Olsen that the DA had closed the investigation into my residency. David Demerjian, chief of the DA's Public Integrity Division, told the

Secret No. 3 – Know Thyself

paper, *Prosecutors had reviewed the matter and determined that it appeared that the councilman did live in the city.*

∽

About a year later I was at a fundraiser for my friend Alan Jackson, who was running for Los Angeles District Attorney. Alan was a first-class prosecutor who'd led the DA's Major Crimes Unit for many years. Alan was also a fellow Air Force veteran and an all-around good dude.

At some point in the evening we were chatting and I mentioned to him that I had been investigated by the DA's office the year before when a retired firefighter had alleged that I did not live in Hermosa Beach. I laughed at the irony that I was supporting him for an office that might have been responsible for prosecuting me just a few months earlier.

Oh, he said, visibly surprised. *That's serious stuff.*

I know, I replied. *But nothing came of it. It's just strange to think there's a file somewhere in your office with my name on it.* Again, I laughed.

Alan didn't crack a smile.

There is, he said. *An investigator probably followed you too. Maybe for a day or so.*

Yikes.

The list of people who'd followed me as a direct result of my vote on the public employees' salary, pension, and benefits had just gotten one person longer.

I wonder if anybody ever attached a GPS to my car?

SECRET No. 4
Pick Your Battles

Politics Is a Contact Sport

I keep asking you why you want to run, and that's not an accident. The nature of the political process is that it requires certainty of its participants. The thing that propels you into this dog-eat-dog arena should be something like whatever propels you through life. Whether it's an impulse to correct some injustice or simply a desire to serve your community, your reason must be rock solid, both for your campaign and your political career.

Why is this so important?

Because at some point during your political career, things will go south. This is a moral certainty.

Maybe you'll contract a case of foot-in-mouth disease (which is sometimes terminal—ask flash-in-the-pan presidential candidate Gary Johnson), or find yourself on the unpopular side of a popular issue. Perhaps your campaign is down to its last dollar at the precise moment your opponent puts out a particularly damaging hit piece, leaving you with few options for a response. These things will happen—they always do—and your reason for entering the political arena must be strong enough to sustain you through the tough times.

Secret No. 4 – Pick Your Battles

Admittedly, there is a certain romanticism to the image of winning an election and waving to the crowd at a ticker-tape parade, but the ego-stroking allure of elected office does not hold up to the grinding work of solving your district's problems. There are moments of glamour, of course, but for every one of those moments there will be another that makes you shake your head and wonder why you even got out of bed that morning. Your reason for running must hold up to those moments. If you're only interested in the prestige, you may want to reconsider. There are simpler, easier ways than political office to satisfy your desire to contribute to your community, like working with nonprofits or volunteering, and they can be terrifically rewarding too.

Once you have decided to make the leap into public life, you need to create a platform, a plan for what you want to do when you get into office. Do you think you can save money somewhere? Are there services you feel can be improved? Are there programs that should be cut? Think about *why* you want to run for office so that you can explain why it will benefit the community.

A hypothetical: Let's say I decide to run for city council because I want to increase the green space in my city and think a good way to do that is by turning one of the main commercial streets into a pedestrian thoroughfare.

As a starting point, it will be important to know what impact converting a street into a pedestrian walkway will have on the city's parking and traffic circulation. Are there examples in neighboring cities I can point to as proof my idea will work? Will local business owners support the plan, even if it means the parking spots directly in front of their businesses will be replaced with sidewalks and bike paths? These are just a few of the basic things to consider, and you'll need to have talking points ready to respond to all of these questions.

Even if you've done the research and have evidence that your idea/plan/proposal is a good one, that doesn't mean it won't run into resistance. Every plan will have detractors, no matter how potentially beneficial it might be to the community. Change can be difficult and will upset people, and it can be particularly upsetting to those who benefit from the status quo. Be prepared for pushback.

For example, when I proposed trimming the city's budget by privatizing Hermosa Beach's traffic enforcement function (i.e., the meter maids), I picked a fight with the public employee unions, the city's finance department, and ultimately (and inadvertently) the police chief. By choosing an issue where I saw an opportunity to reduce the city's costs and improve service to our residents, I threatened some of the city's most entrenched interests.

⸺

The total compensation for some of my city's meter maids (officially called Community Services Officers, or CSOs) was upwards of $94,000 per year. That figure seemed excessive to me, and for a city with limited resources like Hermosa Beach, it presented a prime target for reform.

In fact, when I relayed that salary to residents around town, most reacted by saying: *I should have been a meter maid!* Then some variation of the following conversation would occur.

Incredulous Taxpayer: *What do I need to do to get one of those jobs?*

Me: *First, you have to be able to learn and interpret laws and regulations that relate to parking and animal control.*

Incredulous Taxpayer: *Check that box. I can read.*

Me: *Next, you have to be able to handle large animals.*

Incredulous Taxpayer: *Are large animals an issue in Hermosa Beach?*

Me: *Not normally. Apart from the occasional raccoon or the occasional skunk. One time Erin Andrews tweeted to her two million-plus Twitter followers that a skunk was trapped in the fence behind her house and the city wouldn't help.*

Incredulous Taxpayer: *Wait. THE Erin Andrews? The blonde sportscaster?*

Me: *The same. One of my friends, who follows her on Twitter, asked me why I wasn't helping her with the skunk. I had no idea what he was talking about. I checked my Twitter, saw her tweet, and called the city manager. He had someone from animal control go out and take care of it. Nothing like social media.*

Incredulous Taxpayer: *So what else?*

Me: *You also have to be able to deal with the public and*

drive a stick shift. Oh, and you must have a high school diploma or GED, and a valid Class C driver's license. That's it.

Incredulous Taxpayer: *Amazing.*

Me: *Don't forget the pension. Once you start working for the city you'll be enrolled in the California Public Employee Retirement System. You've heard about it in the news. Most people simply call it CalPERS. Once you're in CalPERS you'll be able to retire at fifty-five and receive 90 percent of your highest one-year salary for the rest of your life.*

The conversation usually ends with the person shaking their head and wondering how a job in which the main skills involve the ability to read, drive a stick shift, and on occasion deal with skunks trapped in a beautiful sportscaster's fence can pay $94,000 a year.

If asked, CSOs would say that salary figure was an exaggeration and that none of them took home more than $61,000 in a year. They would say most CSOs had annual salaries somewhere between $42,000 and $50,000.

If pushed further, they would tell you that dealing with the public can be trying, but they provide an important service and do it very well. They are, as they have taken to calling themselves, "Ambassadors for the City."

And what difference does it matter what CSOs cost, anyway? They're a revenue generator. And they're right. In 2013, the fines and penalties from parking enforcement brought in revenue of approximately $1.7 million for Hermosa Beach—a little less than 10 percent of the city's budget that year.

Secret No. 4 – Pick Your Battles

I attempted to put the city's parking enforcement services out to bid in 2012. The idea was to find out how the market valued the service the CSOs provided. If we could get a fix on the market value of this service, perhaps we could do it with other departments as well.

Moving CSOs off the city's books would end our responsibility for the legacy costs of pensions and benefits that came with them. Excluding salaries, we projected that each of the city's ten CSOs would cost nearly $300,000 in retirement and benefits over the course of their employment with the city, and this estimate was probably too conservative given the skyrocketing increases in healthcare costs. These ten city employees represented nearly $3 million in total direct cost to the city, which came directly out of the general fund.

The general fund is the functional equivalent of a city's checking account, and like any checking account, the more money spent on salaries, pensions, and benefits, the less there was for resurfacing the Little League field or repairing streetlights. Local government is an all-cash business, and spending the city's money on one thing means it can't be spent on another.

This issue was a test case. If we could transition these jobs off the city's books, we might be able to do it with other departments and use the savings for the myriad other things for which we never seemed to have enough money.

At least that was the plan.

Once you've picked your campaign issue(s), take time to study your district's past elections and talk to the people who ran but didn't win. The losers of a race often have a better understanding of what they did wrong than the winners have of what they did right. Victory can seduce a candidate into believing he or she made all the right calls during the campaign, but losers *know* that something went wrong. They're quicker to think critically of their choices, and they're usually eager to sit and talk through the things they'd do differently next time. Learn as much as you can before you begin. Once a political campaign starts, things will move fast and you probably won't have time for calm contemplation.

Remember that most governments focus on a handful of issues: public safety, the budget, green spaces (the environment and parks), and schools. There may be a few boutique issues unique to your district—for instance, Newport Beach, a coastal Orange County city to the south, recently had an election that centered on the use of fire pits on the beach—and these should also be featured prominently in your platform. Whenever you come across a peculiarly local issue, make sure that you understand it and are part of it. In that Newport Beach election, the only people who won were those who campaigned passionately to keep those fire pits. More likely than not, the purely parochial issues will take precedence with local voters.

I knew that when the public saw the $94,000 salary number they would start asking questions. And rightly so. I also knew the answers to those questions were going to be unsatisfactory, and I was looking forward to the debate with the people who would inevitably come forward to defend the CSO compensation packages. I was confident that the public would see the cost was not commensurate with the service and would view the situation for what it was—the bureaucracy defending overpaid union jobs.

I was aware that Newport Beach had already successfully transitioned to private enforcement. Newport's seven-year agreement with their private partner saw the city's revenue increase from $2.8 million to $3.6 million, with a corresponding salary savings of $500,000 *in the first year*. The company that had partnered with Newport was prepared to submit a proposal for Hermosa Beach. They had people and equipment ready to go, and they were so anxious to work with the city that they offered to upgrade our meters and equipment as soon as they took over. It turns out that when profitability is at stake, in-service rates rise and the newest, most modern equipment quickly appears.

The idea was a dead-bang winner. By moving toward a private partnership, we could lower costs, increase revenue, and enhance the service we provided to the public. A report by our new city treasurer David Cohn (remember him?) showed that nearly 10 percent of the city's meters were inoperable or malfunctioning at any given time. The treasurer also reported that nearly $2 million in parking revenue was improperly accounted for each year. By switching to the private partner, Hermosa taxpayers would get more and pay less. Everything augured a victory for more efficient, effective, and smaller government—the Holy Grail for politicians, or at least for conservative ones like me.

Again, that was the plan.

Nine Secrets for Getting Elected

Know Your Opponents

I knew the three public employee union accomplices on the city council would have a Pavlovian response to the alarm bell I was ringing. Gurney Frinks, Cliff Clouseau, and The Man Who Shakes His Head met the proposal with all the enthusiasm of a patient being asked which wisdom tooth they would like to have extracted first. The three rejected the privatization proposal out of hand. I was not concerned about them, though, because the tropes and clichés they would use to defend the union jobs wouldn't resonate with the public. Nobody who worked in the private sector and was subject to California's brutal tax structure could justify those $94,000 salaries.

My analysis was about 95 percent correct.

The one thing I didn't account for, and what ultimately foiled the idea, was vocal public opposition from the Hermosa Beach police chief. According to the chief, the well-paid CSOs were a necessary and important element of the holiest of all policies: public safety.

In May of 2012, the city council was looking at the budget with an eye toward finalizing it by the end of June. The budget process always occurs in the first part of the year, but depending on the status of the city's finances, some years the negotiations are more tedious and intense than others. Because California was still climbing out of the economic crater of 2007–08, 2012 was one of the difficult years.

Neighboring cities were dipping into their reserves and laying off employees to cover budget deficits. The financial storm had not completely passed, but Hermosa Beach managed to keep its head just above the waves. Dealing with a budget deficit in one year was hardly a victory if the same problem would reappear

Secret No. 4 – Pick Your Battles

during the next budget cycle twelve months later. Maintenance could only be deferred for so long before major breakdowns occurred. Potholes could only be patched so many times before the streets needed to be repaved.

But outsourcing meter maids was different.

The reason the CSOs were different was that they fell under the police department's control. They wore uniforms that resembled those worn by our police, and they worked out of the department's building. The meter maids' supervisor was a Hermosa Beach police lieutenant. They were, for all intents and purposes, Hermosa Beach police, and our chief wasn't about to see the size of his department, its budget, or his sphere of control over the city recede.

Instead of providing an objective analysis of the costs and effectiveness of the CSOs, the chief instead retreated into the traditional union stronghold: he insisted the policy change would impair his ability to protect the public and lifted the drawbridge behind him. He gave a dire assessment of the consequences if we employed a private company to do what the CSOs did.

I eventually received a list of 115 separate duties and responsibilities the CSOs performed as proof of their importance to the city's public safety apparatus. These included: #58: *Complete work order sheets for faded signs*; #111: *Assist citizens who are locked out of their vehicles* (don't most people simply call AAA when this happens?); and #115: *Handle animal control calls* (like dealing with angry BBQ-crashing skunks at Erin Andrews' home?)

Each of the 115 different duties and responsibilities the chief identified were tasks any able-bodied worker could perform, requiring no special training. But according to the chief, Hermosa Beach would be a more dangerous place if private sector employees completed work orders for faded signs, collected coins from parking meters, chalked tires, or put tickets on double-parked cars. Because he was the chief, his assessment was more credible than one from one of the pro-union politicians or the meter maids themselves.

The chief knew exactly what he was doing. It was the same tactic used by police unions everywhere: allege that whatever budget cut, restructuring, or reallocation of resources has been proposed will impair public safety. Once the chief weighed in on the issue he also gave political cover to my three colleagues, whose primary interest was in preserving their relationships with employee unions. They no longer had to argue how kind and upstanding the $94,000 meter maids were; they could instead say the cost was justified, whatever it was, because the chief said so.

Truth be told, nobody at city hall knew, or knows, exactly how much the CSOs actually cost.

This is not peculiar to the public sector, since most employees, public or private, probably have little idea what they actually cost their employers after taxes, health benefits, workers' compensation claims, insurance, and the like. Private sector employers cannot pay salaries and benefits beyond what they can actually afford. If they do, they won't be in business long, or their legacy costs will eventually become burdensome and impair their competitiveness. Detroit and the decrepit auto industry towns of the upper Midwest are testaments to the problems that result.

Secret No. 4 – Pick Your Battles

The same constraints do not exist in the public sector, because the taxpayers backstop the government's costs. While I was on the city council, we habitually increased salaries and pensions for public employees with little concern for how our actions would affect the city's future financial health.

Most of my colleagues were comfortable doing this because their political horizon was the next election, which was never more than four years away. It was rare to find elected officials willing to take action today to solve a problem that might not manifest itself for years, or risk the ire and loss of support from the unions at the next election. Elected officials willing to have knock-down-drag-out fights over these issues do exist (in both parties!), and I know many of them, but they are definitely a minority.

In addition to the political incentives for profligacy, CalPERS was the principal factor that kept us from accurately assessing each public employee's true cost. CalPERS is a fiscal enigma wrapped in an accounting riddle that is interpreted by high priests and priestesses from their temple on a remote mountaintop in Sacramento. (The last part of that is not true; I don't know where their temple is.) California's permanent political class jealously guards the entire CalPERS edifice at all levels of government, shaky and unsustainable as it is.

The Same Old Song

A quick primer on CalPERS.

CalPERS was a Depression-era benefit for public employees that was, ironically, a reform measure designed to encourage older workers to retire from public service. At its inception, the pension most public employees received was slightly less than 60 percent of their annual salary. Remember, this was at a time in our history when pensions were relatively unheard of. CalPERS was a progressive advancement for California.

As originally designed, CalPERS would fund public employee pensions from three sources in roughly equal parts: the employee contributed a third, the government contributed a third, and the returns from investments would provide the final piece. But the equation changed over the years, and by the time I was dealing with PERS on the Hermosa Beach City Council, the proportions had shifted so that the public employees contributed zero. Nada. Zip. Zilch. Over the course of many years of negotiations, cities had agreed to pick up that cost in exchange for labor peace.

In 1999 the fiscal dam broke. Or more accurately, Governor Gray Davis broke the dam. Davis made the fateful decision to lower the retirement age from 55 to 50 for police and firefighters and increase the equation for their retirement to 90 percent of their best one-year salary. Now that this standard had been set for state employees, local governments were soon pressured by their police and firefighter unions to follow suit. Of course, Davis was never forced to live with the consequences of this decision because he was defenestrated in the famous 2003 recall election that saw Arnold Schwarzenegger gain the gubernatorial seat.

The problem was that political promises had been made to the public employee unions to pay off Davis' run for governor with money California did not have. The CalPERS board, by now composed almost exclusively of pro-union appointees, promised that their investments could meet the revenue targets necessary to pay the new benefits.

Secret No. 4 – Pick Your Battles

Until recently, CalPERS operated on the assumption that it would generate an 8 percent return on investment (ROI). The CalPERS board recently voted to reduce that assumption to 7 percent. Anyone with a 401(k) knows 7 percent return year-in and year-out is fantasy, including former New York City Mayor Michael Bloomberg. When asked about his city's pension system and its 7 percent assumed rate of return, he said: "If somebody offers you a guaranteed 7 percent on your money for the rest of your life, you take it and just make sure the guy's name is not Madoff."[6] Most funds set the conservative estimated rate of return somewhere closer to 3 percent per year. Using 7 percent assumptions in a 3 percent world means eventually being forced to make up the difference with money from somewhere. Cities all over the state are forced to make tough choices when Sacramento math becomes a local reality, and I'm sure you can guess where the money ultimately comes from.

When the promises outstripped financial reality, the CalPERS board was forced to chase returns. Of course, the highest returns are typically associated with the riskiest propositions (it's that risk versus reward thing), and CalPERS soon found itself invested in things like collateralized debt obligation (CDO). You may remember CDOs from the subprime mortgage crisis. Or perhaps you've heard them referred to by their more common name: toxic mortgages.

The timing of Davis' promise to the public safety unions was also important. Remember, his great leap forward in CalPERS benefits occurred at the height of the dot-com boom. Silicon

---

[6] Mary Williams Walsh and Danny Hakim, "Public Pensions Faulted for Bets on Rosy Returns," *The New York Times* (May 27, 2012).

Valley was awash in money, and the tax revenue flowed up I-80 from Silicon Valley to Sacramento and filled the state's coffers.

The consequences of unrealistic promises made during the boom unspooled in the predictable way when the dot-com bubble burst. Unable to find the money it needed in the marketplace, CalPERS sent bills to cities to make up the difference between the money required to pay the promised benefits at the fairytale 7 percent rate of return and the money the state actually had. California's assembly members felt little compunction about shaking down cities in their home districts when Sacramento needed the money.

The bills CalPERS sent blew fire truck–sized holes in city budgets. Pension obligations and the state's demands helped bankrupt cities like San Bernardino, Vallejo, and Stockton.

Hermosa Beach's CalPERS obligations didn't sink the city, but it was taking on water and listing badly. In 2008–09, the city contributed just under $5 million of an approximate $26 million budget for pension obligations. That's 18 percent of the city's total budget. Four years later, that number increased to $6 million. By 2018, the cost is estimated to be 23 percent of the city's total budget.

To paraphrase a former Los Angeles county supervisor, Hermosa Beach was rapidly becoming a retirement program for government employees that provided services to its residents on the side.

The average California taxpayer is unlikely to be concerned that the CalPERS board of directors missed its targeted rate of return this year, or about the ramifications of that failure for their city's finances. The public is prevented from focusing on

Secret No. 4 – Pick Your Battles

this problem by its complexity, the ubiquitous jargon, and the fact it is so difficult to communicate CalPERS concepts clearly. The exclusivity of the CalPERS lingo also makes it easier for those with an interest in the system's continuation to dismiss those who don't.

You think CalPERS has problems? they say. *No, it's fine. You just don't understand.*

⌒

Running for office is a little like singing a song. And just as every song needs a chorus, every campaign needs a good message. A capable opponent will try to get you out of your comfort zone, away from the issues you've prepared, and into territory that makes you stutter and misspeak. Your opponents will do everything they can to get you to change your tune.

Remember Gary Johnson? For about two weeks during the 2016 presidential election the New Mexico libertarian was the darling of the disgruntled on both sides of the political spectrum (or perhaps the people in the middle?), largely because of his fluency on domestic issues.

Johnson was gaining traction, and some observers thought he might present the same out-of-nowhere option to the right that Senator Bernie Sanders was presenting to the left.

And then the question happened.

Asked by an MSNBC interviewer what he would do about the humanitarian crisis in the Syrian city of Aleppo, Johnson responded: *What is Aleppo?*

Nobody heard much from Gary Johnson after that. His

embarrassment was a lesson for all would-be politicians. Your job is to take whatever is thrown at you and bring it back to your core message. It doesn't matter what the question is; your answer should always return to whatever song you want to sing.

An example concerning President Donald Trump offers a stark contrast to Gary Johnson. At a New Year's celebration with a throng of reporters crowded around him, one called out to the president-elect: *Mr. Trump! What is your New Year's resolution?*

Innocuous as it appears, this was a potentially hazardous question. Mr. Trump could have responded in any number of ways, lots of them not good, and if he said something off-color or impolitic, the press would have had a field day with it. But he didn't. In fact, you already know what he said, even if you haven't heard his answer.

Without skipping a beat, the president-elect responded: *To make America great again.*

Where It All Went Wrong

A Hermosa Beach CSO—let's call her Officer Laverne—was patrolling the northern part of Hermosa Beach at 10:30 a.m. on August 8, 2007. Like most of the city, the northern part is densely populated, and there are always fewer parking spaces available than there are cars that want them. This is partly due to the city's haphazardly planned growth over the years, and partly due to the crush of visitors to the beach on one of Hermosa's patented sunny summer days.

On this particular Wednesday morning, Officer Laverne was patrolling the streets in her three-wheeled go-cart when she

Secret No. 4 – Pick Your Battles

came across a resident washing his car in his driveway. In the northern part of the city there are some older homes with very, very small garages. Some of these homes abut the public right of way (also the product of the city's decades of poorly planned growth). Because the resident couldn't wash his car in his shoebox garage, he had pulled it partway out, thereby blocking the sidewalk. This was the only way he could wash his car without having some portion of it sticking out into the street. The street is also narrow, and as it was a sunny summer day, it was full of parked cars. Had he put his car in the street to wash it, no one would have been able to pass.

For a resident to place his car halfway across the sidewalk is verboten under the city's municipal code, and task number 24 of the 115 CSO duties and responsibilities list was "Vehicle tows for blocking driveways." When Officer Laverne happened upon the resident, she told him to move his car.

(Obviously, I was not there for the discussion, so please read the following as a literary reenactment of events.)

Officer Laverne: *Sir, you can't wash your car in your driveway.*

It's easy to imagine the resident's response to this. It's a midsummer morning, and the resident is standing in his driveway, a garden hose in one hand, being told by Officer Laverne, a so-called City Ambassador, that he was breaking the law.

Resident: *Sorry. Right. It's okay. This is my car, and it's my driveway. I'll be done in a minute.*

Officer Laverne: *It's still illegal, sir. You need to move your car.*

Resident: *Oh, gosh. I didn't know this was illegal. I don't have room to put the car anywhere else. It's too dangerous to wash the car in the street, and nobody could get by if I did, but okay. How about you make another loop on your rounds, and I'll be done before you get back. No harm, no foul.*

Officer Laverne: *Sir, I need you to move the car now or I'll have to ticket you.*

At this point, the resident homeowner was probably looking around for Ashton Kutcher and his *Punk'd* camera crew, and decided to continue washing his car. It was his car. It was also his driveway. A man's house is his castle and all that.

But Officer Laverne, operationally part of the Hermosa Beach police department and deputized a vital public safety officer by the chief of police, persisted with the enforcement of task number 24. This rule applied even if the person blocking the driveway owned it. This, as they say, is the moment where things went south.

But before we finish this story, let's stop for a quick observation and a question.

The question first: If Officer Laverne were working for a private company instead of the Hermosa Beach police department, would this situation have escalated? I'd lay even odds the answer to that question is no. But because Officer Laverne was driving in a cart with emergency lights on the top, and because

Secret No. 4 – Pick Your Battles

she wore a uniform like our police, and because she worked for the police department, her attitude was more akin to that of law enforcement than that of a city ambassador.

This attitude is not peculiar to meter maids. I cringe whenever I see regular police officers in tactical gear that makes them indistinguishable from soldiers, because if you dress like a soldier then you're more likely to act like a soldier.

I remember the first time I was deployed to Italy with my fighter squadron in the early 1990s. I was uncomfortable at the sight of young, stern, and impressively well-armed members of the Carabinieri (the Italian national paramilitary police, once used by Mussolini to suppress his opposition) casually walking around the public squares. Like many Americans, I had never before seen police with automatic weapons in public. Nobody in the US ever saw a police officer with a submachine gun slung over their shoulder like the ones I saw walking around the edges of the Italian plazas. But the Italian public insouciantly strolled with their half-size Dixie cups of gelato, their kids in strollers, as if the men wearing peaked caps and smart black uniforms carrying submachine guns were invisible. But I noticed. I think the sight of military men with automatic weapons in public places makes most Americans uncomfortable. And it says much about us as a nation that it does.

Back to the uniforms. Do they make a difference? By themselves, no. But we all know that the way people dress does affect the way the world perceives them and how people perceive themselves. And perceptions shape actions.

As a young lieutenant in the Air Force, I worked for a short time on the commanding general's staff in the headquarters building, where most wore the standard blue Air Force uniform. On the flight line where I normally worked, out in the elements, it was loud, hot, and dangerous, and it smelled like jet fuel. Airmen wore fatigues (then called battle dress uniforms, or BDUs in Air Force speak) or flight suits. The general, a fighter pilot by trade, knew that the people in the headquarters building sometimes forgot that the Air Force's mission was out on the flight line and not in the offices where the file cabinets were. So every week he ordered a "Warrior Day," when everyone in the headquarters had to wear their BDUs or flight suits. The general thought there was something to it. I did too. It reminded everyone what we were all ultimately there to do.

My observation is that the converse is also true: If meter maids dress like the police, chances are they're going to be more prone to act like the police. And if police officers dress like soldiers, guess what? They will act more like soldiers. When we put our meter maids into police-like uniforms and treat them like police and supervise them with police, no one should be surprised when someone who has forgotten to curb the wheels on their car is transformed from a person who didn't park correctly into a perp.

According to the later-filed criminal complaint, Officer Laverne alleged that the resident assaulted her by grabbing her arm and spraying her with his garden hose when she confronted him about his parking violation. Faced with an aggressive perp, she did what any law enforcement officer would do and called for backup. A few minutes later, not one, two, three, or four but *FIVE* of Hermosa Beach's finest showed up to help Officer Laverne keep a taxpaying resident from washing his car in his own driveway.

After some consultation, the officers advised Officer Laverne to file a complaint against the resident for spraying her with his hose. She did, and the resident was subsequently taken into custody.

I placed him under arrest and put him in the back seat of my police car and drove him to the station, said the arresting Hermosa Beach police officer.

The resident elaborated on being placed under arrest. He told me the officers forcibly put him facedown on the ground and cuffed him. The resident said he even got the obligatory head bump on the side of the car on his way into the back seat, just like you see on cop shows. The resident told me he stayed in the city's jail for seven hours before a friend came with the $500 bail.

All the words you just read are true. A Hermosa Beach resident was taken into custody by five police officers, a CSO, and her supervisor, for allegedly squirting a hose at a meter maid who wanted him to stop washing his car on the sidewalk in front of his own driveway.

Being cuffed and put in jail for the better part of a day would seem enough punishment for unlawfully parking one's car. But the madness, unfortunately, did not end there. The point was not yet sufficiently made, and the police had the city prosecutor file a criminal complaint against this resident. Worse still, the case actually went to trial.

After a two-day trial (May 30, 2008 and June 3, 2008), the jury in the criminal matter correctly identified this case as patently ridiculous. A jury of twelve of the alleged hose-squirting resident's peers listened to the evidence and argument, and after deliberating for twelve minutes, found him not guilty of any of the charges. As it turned out, the other responding police officers (now placed under oath) did not remember Officer Laverne's uniform being wet or rumpled, and there was some confusion as to whether she had ever dismounted her scooter to confront the resident at all. What would you think if you were made to miss work for two days to hear this case as a juror? Right, me too. That wasn't the end.

Vindicated, but out $45,000 in attorneys' fees, the resident was righteously incensed and did what most people would do: he sued the city. On August 3, 2009, the resident filed a civil rights action against the City of Hermosa Beach, Officer Laverne, and her supervisors in the police department "in an amount according to proof at trial." Sorry, that's legalese. The English translation for that phrase is, *whatever a jury of Los Angeles County voters thinks I deserve for being treated like this by the City of Hermosa Beach for washing my car in front of my own driveway in the middle of the morning.* The resident claimed the CSO officer was improperly trained, and because she was supervised by the police department, the city was liable.

With his "not guilty" verdict from the criminal trial in hand, we were off to the races. So were the lawyers. The federal statutes are correctly designed to punish those who trample the civil rights of others, and one little-known aspect of the law (at least among non-lawyers) is that when the plaintiff prevails in a civil rights action the government has to pay his attorneys' fees. In Los Angeles, plaintiffs' lawyers commonly bill at $1,000 or even more per hour. (That's a little more than $16 per minute.) Add to the expense the cost of expert witnesses (who testified on such things as the proper use of force by the officers, Officer Laverne's

Secret No. 4 – Pick Your Battles

training or lack thereof, and plaintiff's injuries at similar hourly rates), and soon the legal costs outstrip whatever damage the plaintiff recovers. And because Officer Laverne was employed by the City of Hermosa Beach, guess who was on the hook for all of it? *Ding-ding!* If you said the taxpayers, run to the kitchen and get yourself a cookie.

When the city council first learned of the resident's lawsuit, there was a natural inclination on the part of staff and city council *to defend our people*, so the lawsuit progressed. Not too far into it, our lawyers (civil lawyers, not the prosecutors who lost the jury trial) advised the city council that the case was an absolute dog and we were going to lose bigger than Sunday. And when we lost, we were going to end up paying both the plaintiff's damages and attorneys' fees. After some very preliminary legal wrangling we paid the resident approximately $100,000 and put to rest a case that should have ended with a polite discussion on a Wednesday morning two years prior between a meter maid and a homeowner on the sidewalk in front of his home.

A final note: the CSO who put us in this situation soon after this went out on paid medical leave and then took a job elsewhere.

SECRET No. 5

Be Prepared for the Ridiculousness

Canaries in the Political Coal Mine

Political gadflies. Every town has them. They are politically active people who have no official role and hold no office. They come to city council meetings and aren't shy about sounding off on whatever issues are important to them, relevant or not. Their contributions are often off-topic and time-consuming, but occasionally they will add value by providing facts or perspective to the topic at hand. On occasion, their input and influence will move policy decisions in unexpected—and unwelcome—directions. As you will soon see, gadflies are almost always colorful characters, too.

Example 1: Dr. D.

Dr. D. was an older gentleman, always clad in pressed khakis and a button-down Oxford, who for a time would appear at city council meetings and advocate for "European-style" sunbathing on a portion of our public beach. I suspect Dr. D. was mainly interested in having a topless beach in Hermosa, but when I pressed him on this point he assured me he would take full advantage of the new rules too.

Oh, joy.

Secret No. 5 – Be Prepared for the Ridiculousness

Always straight-faced, he would come to the podium during the public comment period of our city council meetings and extol the benefits of "European-style" sunbathing. He told us it would improve the health of visitors to our beach (they'd get more vitamin D) and could be a marketing angle to set us apart from neighboring cities. *Think of all the Europeans who visit Los Angeles every year,* he said. *They would all come to Hermosa Beach!*

Dr. D. was persistent and apparently serious in his belief that being *au naturel* on our beach was a really, really good idea.

The city council patiently listened to him, but today bathing suits are still required apparel on Hermosa Beach.

Dr. D. was harmless, and there was a 0.0 percent chance that his idea was going to catch hold with Hermosa Beach residents or anyone on the city council. This was a relief, because I couldn't imagine presiding over the official ribbon-cutting (or is it a towel-dropping?) if Dr. D.'s idea had ever gotten any momentum.

Example 2: Beecher

Whenever the approval for a new restaurant was on the city council agenda, a resident we'll call Beecher would appear at the podium, wearing his brightly colored tropical shirts, to calmly recite crime statistics for the city council and the public at home. Reading glasses perched at the tip of his angular nose, Beecher would lean into the microphone and warn of the perils our community faced if we approved any more alcohol outlets in our little beach city. Devil rum, the people who drank it, and the places that sold it were eroding the quality of life in our city, he said.

Unlike Dr. D., Beecher was serious, thoughtful, and articulate, and his persistence over time had gained a contingent of sympathetic residents who were tired of Hermosa Beach being overrun by booze-fueled twenty-something partygoers every weekend. His position as self-appointed leader of the city's small-but-vocal group of prohibitionists might have carried more weight with the city council, however, if he hadn't once been arrested for climbing into the back of a parked police car, drunk as a pledge-week freshman and looking for a place to nap. As it was, he found dozens of ways to undercut himself.

Regardless of what the city council thought of Beecher's arguments or character, he was an advocate for a specific issue that was a concern for a not-inconsequential portion of our community. It's important not to ignore gadflies like Beecher, because on occasion he identified issues that would catch hold with city council members and other members of the community. Beecher was a voice, and one worth listening to—*sometimes*.

EXAMPLE 3: ANTI-OIL EVANGELICA

Every now and again, there are gadflies like Anti-Oil Evangelica. As you will see, she was a canary in the political coal mine—and the issues and concerns she voiced were clear warnings about hazards ahead.

Dreams and Ambition

Buddy Brewer (not his real name) was a young man with a dream, and like many young men, his dream included beer. In the summer of 2010, Buddy wanted to open his own microbrewery and was exploring the possibility of setting up shop in Hermosa Beach's tiny industrial park. A veteran of the microbrewery industry, Buddy penciled out the operation and thought that he could run a profitable microbrewery producing around three thousand barrels of beer annually (one barrel of beer equals two kegs). The operation Buddy had in mind was not going to put Anheuser-Busch out of business. At least not yet.

Like all entrepreneurs, Buddy planned on starting small but had a vision of something bigger. His idea was to start a local brand. *Once I get my foot in the door,* he told us at a city council meeting, *I'll open up a plant. But I'll still put on my label 'Brewed in Hermosa Beach.'*

He wanted the first shop to be in the city where he'd grown up. *That's why I'm here,* he said, *to live my dreams.*

The first thing he needed was a place in town where he could put a microbrewery. Hermosa Beach is a 1.4-square-mile city that is almost entirely built-out, but it does have one small, industrially zoned area near the city yard. Size constraints caused the area to be chronically underutilized. Buddy found space, but there was no provision in the zoning code for a microbrewery. Buddy would have to get special permission from the city to open his business there.

This shouldn't be a problem, Buddy thought, because bakeries were on the list, and the component processes for a microbrewery were similar to a bakery's. Furthermore, a surfboard maker and auto paint shop were already there, and those industries were much more impactful to the environment and community than anything Buddy intended to do.

Wort? That Just Sounds Bad

The lack of an express provision allowing microbreweries in the zoning code was not an insurmountable problem. The city's code allowed the planning director (the city's top land use official) to make what is called a "similar use determination" and find that the microbrewery was equivalent to the other uses already approved for that zone. It was a wonderfully efficient process for accommodating odds-and-ends situations like this that occasionally arose, and it vested the city's head planning official with the ability to make a quick decision so that entrepreneurs could pursue the American Dream.

The planning director reviewed the zoning code and agreed with Buddy that a microbrewery was conformable with the other businesses already allowed in the industrial park. At the city council meeting on July 13, 2010, the planning director recommended the city council approve a resolution that would permit microbreweries in the industrial zone.

Councilman Cliff Clouseau disagreed. A prohibitionist with the demeanor of an Amish undertaker, he strongly opposed any form of alcohol being brewed in his town. He also objected to the odors that might be emitted from fermentation, and voiced specific concern about "wort."

Wort is the unfortunate name of a by-product of the brewing process, and Cliff Clouseau was convinced that having it lying about would create an unbearable odor for the neighbors. Wort just sounded like it smelled bad, and Cliff Clouseau wanted to know what the microbrewery planned to do about it.

So did Anti-Oil Evangelica. An outwardly pleasant woman probably in her mid- to late-sixties, Anti-Oil Evangelica used the same tone when she addressed the city council that an eighth-grade English teacher might use after she found her class had misbehaved with a substitute. Whenever she rose to speak, I half expected her to end her comments with a schoolmarmish threat of "consequences" if we didn't shape up. As her name suggests, she would be back in two years with her curt tone and pixie cut aflame over the prospect of oil derricks, pipelines, and natural gas fumes within a few blocks of her home. But for now she was focused on the possibility that the light industrial park might be used for light industrial purposes.

The problem is that once you allow one business in, she told us at one council meeting, *you get more.*

∽

Specifically, Anti-Oil Evangelica was in a rabid lather about smells from the microbrewery that might migrate into her home. She lived west of the industrial zone, but on occasion the winds shifted from east to west, and when they did, Anti-Oil Evangelica was forced to close her windows. Of course this was a climatological rarity, since winds blowing from east to west on the California coast meant they were blowing from the land out to sea.

Buddy was also at that meeting, and to his credit, he calmly listened to Cliff Clouseau and Anti-Oil Evangelica trying to torpedo his dream. When he rose to speak, he told the city council that wort wasn't nearly as bad as it sounded; it was actually nothing more than cooked, processed grain. When the brewing was complete he would sell the stuff to a company that would in turn sell it to farmers, who used it to feed their livestock. Almost nothing of what he used to brew beer went to waste. *It was actually quite a green process,* he said.

This rational answer displeased Cliff Clouseau, who turned his attention back to the planning director.

Wouldn't it be better just to put a completely green business where the microbrewery would be? Surely there was a business willing to do something more green than cooking wort and making beer, wasn't there?

Maybe, the planning director said, *but those types of businesses probably wouldn't be listed in the zoning code either. Green or not, the city council would have to specially approve them.*

Humph.

⁓

At the end of the debate on July 13, 2010, the city council declined to follow the planning director's recommendation that microbreweries were functionally similar to the other light industrial uses already in the park.

A new small business would have been born.

Instead, our decision condemned Buddy to his own personal City Hall Odyssey. I apologized to him from the dais for condemning him to a slow and lingering death when we made the decision. Because three city council members were concerned about the smell of wort, a young man who wanted to start a small business in his hometown was cast into the Pit of Administrative Despair, and just like the Pit of Despair in *The Princess Bride*, ours came complete with its own life-sucking machine. The main difference between the movie version and the administrative one was that the people and businesses we hooked our machine to paid us to operate it. The cost came out of their pockets, which was something like making a condemned person pay for their last meal and firing squad.

Instead of securing investors, sampling hops, and buying vats and boilers, Buddy would spend the next six months on a paperwork steeplechase around city hall. If he was able to successfully negotiate the planning commission and city staff, then and only then would he be able to return and ask permission to open a small business in his hometown.

The Quest for Approval

The first stop on Buddy's City Hall Odyssey was the Hermosa Beach planning commission.

The planning commission functions in much the same way a legislative committee would in Congress. Just as the House Budget Committee works out the details before the budget is presented to the full House for a vote, the planning commission deals with land use issues before they are presented to the city council. California's thicket of environmental laws, its exacting and Byzantine building codes, and Hermosa Beach's own requirements made the building and planning process difficult. The planning commission takes a first cut at these issues, and unless we choose to formally review their determinations, their judgment on them is final.

As good as the planning commission was, there wasn't any reason for them to be involved here. Formulating land use policies for Hermosa Beach was squarely within the city council's purview. The planning director applied the zoning code to the facts and arrived at a very reasonable conclusion: brewing beer was functionally equivalent to baking bread.

The problem, of course, was that Gurney Frinks, Cliff Clouseau, and The Man Who Shakes His Head (TMWSHH) didn't want to have a microbrewery in town. But they had no good reason to reject it.

Cliff Clouseau and Gurney Frinks were concerned about being labeled antibusiness, and my colleagues did not want to publicly reject the new business. Cliff Clouseau, Gurney Frinks, and TMWSHH were a majority on the five-member council, and they had the votes to do what they wanted, but when they did things that were overtly antibusiness I made sure to highlight it to the press and public. They hated that. So their challenge was to find a technicality that would kill off this prospective business, but do it quietly. They were going to use the city's administrative process against Buddy's prospective business in the same way Dr. Kevorkian might use an otherwise fluffy and comfortable pillow on one of his patients.

A majority of the city council voted to do what elected officials at all levels do when they want to avoid making a tough or unpopular decision—they sought political cover in the process. Instead of making the policy decision that we didn't want microbreweries in our industrial park, we instead passed the question downward to our appointed (read: unelected) planning commission. Given the state of California's environmental laws alone, with enough time and scrutiny the planning commission could find a hatful of reasons for us to disallow almost any prospective enterprise from starting up in the city. My disapproving colleagues could examine the planning commission's recommendation like Hamlet holding Yorick's skull, and after grave consideration would conclude that microbreweries would present traffic circulation/parking/greenhouse emissions/noise/operating hours/carbon neutrality issues they simply couldn't ignore. The planning commission would supply the reason(s) for elected officials to avoid doing what they never wanted to do in the first place.

Politically Expedient Hidey-Holes

The planning commission took up the matter on September 21, 2010, a mere three months after the city council had assigned it to them for review.

The city staff extensively researched microbreweries, their ventilation systems, and the environmental impacts of the brewing process. At the public meeting a city planner outlined a list of recommended administrative requirements for the new business, including waste and recycling plans, water minimization and reuse plans, and traffic mitigation plans. Additionally, if the planning commission decided to permit microbreweries, the businesses would also have to perform an assessment of greenhouse gasses in the areas of materials, wastewater, energy, and transportation. This, the deputy city planner assigned to the project flatly noted, was the first time the city had applied provisions of the municipal code concerning greenhouse gas emissions to a new business. Lucky for Buddy and his microbrewery.

One of the commissioners wanted to know more. *What other things are they going to look into, in terms of environment?* he asked.

Well it would be odors. And dust from raw materials like grains, and so forth, the deputy city planner said.

If the city decided to allow this type of business into the

industrial zone, the brewery would have to employ an enclosed recycling system.

I've spoken to a number of experts at universities, the erstwhile deputy city planner said, *and a self-contained system was the best way to contain any smell.* The planner did not specify which university or which department, or the expert with whom she had spoken, but one can only imagine what equipment and processes a PhD at UCLA might suggest for making an industrial operation completely odorless. It wasn't going to be cheap.

Anti-Oil Evangelica was also at the planning commission meeting. She hoped the commission would conduct a thorough investigation of the proposed beer-making enterprise. She didn't want them to do research; she wanted an *investigation*, as if Vito Corleone were trying to open a local branch of the GenCo Olive Oil Company in the industrial park. Anti-Oil Evangelica was going to come to every commission meeting to make sure the investigation was completed.

Anti-Oil Evangelica also asked the commissioners to pay particular attention to the odors a microbrewery might generate. *A business like that is going to emit an odor of some kind,* she said. Popcorn does not emit an odor, nor does freshly cut timber. Odors result from unpleasantness, like a gym bag full of sweaty workout clothes forgotten in the trunk. Her word choice was deliberate.

On the other hand, the existing surfboard shop in the industrial zone, which used resins to make surfboards, was different. *We're very proud that this is Hermosa Beach, and we're known for surfing,* she said. Resins used to make surfboards were not

Secret No. 5 – Be Prepared for the Ridiculousness

the same as cooking cereal grains because Anti-Oil Evangelica apparently liked surfing. She did not like beer.

Once the commission and city staff were finished, Buddy got the chance to speak. *I don't know where to start,* he said, exasperated.

Buddy explained that what people were calling odors were not odors at all. The smell a microbrewery produced, he said, was *like Grape-Nuts steeped in warm water*. He also compared it to the smell of oatmeal, which, if true, means kitchens all over the world are subjected to this noxious odor daily.

Buddy wasn't going to blanket Anti-Oil Evangelica's neighborhood with the smell of warm Grape-Nuts every day. *My brewing schedule at maximum capacity would be two ninety-minute brews a day, every fourth day.* In other words, the neighbors would be exposed to the smell of warm Grape-Nuts steeped in warm water for a maximum of three hours each week. Assuming his brewing schedule coincided with the wind blowing from east to west, that is.

Hermosa Beach already had a restaurant that brewed its own beer using almost the exact same system Buddy would likely use if his business were allowed to go forward.

I've hit a brick wall, the young entrepreneur said.

The Final Showdown

The planning commission took up the matter again about a month later, on October 19, 2010. Environmental laws required the planning commission to conduct a second public hearing to allow the public sufficient time to review the environmental report for the change in the zoning code. But for this statutory requirement, the meeting on September 21 would have sufficed.

It was short and to the point. Two commissioners opposed the idea of having microbreweries in the light industrial zone, and two of them believed the use was consistent with the uses already there. The fifth commissioner recused himself because he lived within five hundred feet of the proposed site, which left the commission in a 2-2 deadlock.

Three months, two planning commission meetings, and countless staff hours later, no new light had been shed on the subject of microbreweries in the light industrial zone. The planning commission returned the issue, like a re-gifted present, to the city council.

༄

Five months after the issue originally arose, the issue returned to the city council for further debate on December 14, 2010.

Cliff Clouseau returned to the idea of a green enterprise zone. Brewing beer, even in small quantities, was not a green endeavor in his opinion. *What about the carbon footprint?* he asked. But this too went nowhere. He relinquished the floor to Gurney Frinks.

My biggest concern, Gurney Frinks began, *is odors.*

The city staff told Gurney it had researched the issue, and technology would mitigate the problem to a level of insignificance.

But what specific technology is he going to use? Gurney Frinks asked.

Secret No. 5 – Be Prepared for the Ridiculousness

There is no applicant yet, the planning director respectfully reminded the councilman. *This is just approval of the ordinance that would allow the microbrewery to exist.* At this stage, the question was purely hypothetical.

Gurney Frinks nodded. He was awake, his eyes were open, and he was apparently listening. He then repeated the exact same question. Frinks' question was the equivalent of the city council discussing the terms of a taxi franchise ordinance and wanting to know what grade of motor oil the taxis would use.

TMWSHH stepped up to the plate next. What followed was a question-and-answer session with the planning director that would shake the faith of the heartiest defender of the democratic process.

Can you tell me how this is going to strengthen the economic base of the city? Is there an economic gain by this coming into town? TMWSHH asked the planning director.

One beat. Two beats. Like any good straight man, the planning director didn't want to step on TMWSHH's punch line. Like everyone else who heard it, he assumed the question was a setup for something else yet to come.

But TMWSHH didn't finish the joke.

Certainly—it's a vacant building, the planning director cautiously answered. There was no business there. Any new business would, by definition, add to commerce and the city's tax base.

No, that just makes the landlord happy, TMWSHH responded.

Buddy probably started wondering how he would like brewing beer in Reno or Austin.

But the punch line never came. TMWSHH was serious, so the planning director tried again.

Employment. It brings people to the city.

The planning director was being asked to explain at a public meeting how the addition of a business where none existed was an economic gain for the city. This was eighth grade civics.

TMWSHH was not a good student. *Well, that's a very general statement,* he said.

Sadly, this may have been the intellectual peak of the city council's deliberations.

When the three councilmen were done, the mayor invited Buddy to address the city council. Undaunted, the young man sallied forth and took his place at the podium.

Still naively operating under the assumption that the council was simply misinformed, he tried to provide information that would show my colleagues there was nothing to fear from his business. A microbrewery wasn't going to ruin the neighborhood. He tried to make his point by comparing Hermosa Beach with the Anchor Brewing Company in San Francisco. That brewery had been in existence since 1897 and was situated between a school and church in a densely populated neighborhood on Potrero Hill. He testified that the neighborhood where Anchor is located is demographically similar to Hermosa Beach. He showed aerial photographs of Anchor's brewery and the buildings around it, which included a church and a school. Buddy had gone so far as to actually call the school and the church to ask if they had any problems with their beer-making neighbor. Neither had any complaints.

Buddy told us Anchor produced 228 barrels of beer daily. If the council allowed microbreweries in Hermosa Beach, his operation would produce only 30 barrels per day.

In direct response to TMWSHH's question about the

Secret No. 5 – Be Prepared for the Ridiculousness

"economic base" of the start-up, Buddy told us he would employ three people at maximum production. Those three people would work at a business in a space that was currently empty. Of course Buddy was too polite and deferential to say that, but he should have.

After his presentation, the young entrepreneur agreed to take questions from the dais, where the following dialogue occurred:

Cliff Clouseau: *You described the smell as a sweet grain smell. Is that correct?*

Buddy: *I describe it to everybody as a bowl of Grape-Nuts: add water, and microwave.*

Cliff Clouseau: [Leaning forward, pen twirling between index and forefinger. It was apparent from his demeanor that he thought the trap was being set.] *Ah, the Grape-Nuts analogy. That it would smell no different than a microwaved bowl of Grape-Nuts.*

Buddy: *Correct.*

Cliff Clouseau: *So, that's not very impactful, right? That smell?*

Buddy: *Um . . .*

Cliff Clouseau: *I've tried the experiment. Does it change the smell of Grape-Nuts by microwaving it?*

When I heard this, I smiled inside at the thought of Cliff Clouseau hovered over the microwave like a mad scientist conducting an experiment. I wondered if he altered the size of the bowls or the amount of water hoping to find just the right combination that would turn the cereal's smell from cooked grain into burnt hair. I smiled again at the thought of his disappointment when the Grape-Nuts refused to smell like anything other than cooked Grape-Nuts.

> Buddy: *No, it doesn't. The cereal grains, the barley, the wheat, it's the same grain.*
>
> Cliff Clouseau: *The comparison, the analogy that it's compatible with, say, a bakery . . . but it's not baking; it's fermentation.*
>
> Buddy: *Correct. But it doesn't go airborne.*

If Cliff Clouseau had done even a cursory amount of research before the meeting with Buddy, he would have discovered that the ovens used for industrial baking are not self-contained like the vats used for fermentation. Brewing beer is necessarily a closed-loop process, and not much vapor or smell escapes. Instead of doing research, Clouseau spent time preparing for this moment attempting to do Grape-Nut alchemy in his kitchen.

> Cliff Clouseau: *Well, that's another point I wanted to make. There are two issues: There's the odor from the brewing of the beer, and there's the problem with the residue, the mash. I understand you haul that out to farmers for their livestock. That's wonderful, but they're not standing there with a shovel as the process is going on. There's a period when the mash is sitting around.*

Buddy: *No.*

Cliff Clouseau: *Never? Not at all?*

The words spilled forth with the same mixture of disbelief and sarcasm he would have used if Buddy had told him George W. Bush was a graduate of Yale and Harvard Business School.

Buddy: *Federally, it is not allowed to stay on-site indoors. It can go outdoors in a trash enclosure, but it cannot stay on-site past the day it is generated.*

Cliff Clouseau: *Is that trash enclosure hermetically sealed so no odors escape? None?*

Buddy: *No, it's not. But what's the difference between that and a restaurant trash can?*

Cliff Clouseau: [Stuttering] *Well, you're right. There are restaurant trash cans that I have objections with too.* [More stuttering] *But . . . I'm just saying, that, that, I'm just saying, the number of odors, it's just, it just seems to me disingenuous to sort of characterize this as a bowl of Grape-Nuts. There is an odor. Am I wrong?*

Buddy: *There is an odor created. I'm not going to deny that. I would say it's pleasant. I like to eat the mash after it's done because it's like eating grainy, fiber sweet cereal. It's delicious. They make pretzels out of it. They make dog biscuits. There are a lot of uses for spent grain. It doesn't stay on-site.*

Cliff Clouseau dejectedly furled his bright green antibusiness battle flag and quit.

Gurney Frinks was next. Still focused on the vapor recovery system, he asked Buddy to elaborate on what he would use to recover emissions from the microbrewery.

The prospective brewer responded with a technical explanation of the system he would likely use and submerged Frinks in more detail about the mechanics of brewing than he could possibly follow. Realizing he could no longer touch his toes to the bottom of the analytical pool, Frinks changed the conversation.

What about noises? Would the clinking of bottles make a lot of noise?

The main noise is a grain mill, Buddy said, *which is two rollers on a four horsepower motor that smashes grain. Really not a whole lot of noise.* (Lawn mowers use larger engines.)

Also unable to extract a confession that Buddy was surreptitiously trying to destroy the neighborhood, Gurney Frinks passed the baton—or more accurately, the cudgel—to The Man Who Shakes His Head. TMWSHH's first question was about what had transpired at the planning commission.

This came before the planning commission, and I don't think you attended that meeting, correct?

The question betrayed that TMWSHH was unaware the commission held two meetings, and he had only watched the second one. Buddy had gone to both.

I was here.

Did you testify at that meeting?

Buddy responded truthfully that he had not testified at the

October 19 meeting. There was no reason for him to. The issue had been discussed in detail at the meeting prior.

I've never been to a planning commission meeting, he said. *This is my second council meeting, and I didn't know when I was allowed to speak.*

I'm a little miffed at that, TMWSHH said. *We've spent a tremendous amount of money on this as a city, at our expense, not yours, to maybe allow this usage, and I'm kind of amazed that you weren't up there, and I wasn't sure if we should continue this process.*

TMWSHH said the words as if Buddy was the one who was causing us all to undergo this process, like someone who plans a dinner party and then shows up late.

Like Cliff Clouseau, TMWSHH was gearing up to lead the young entrepreneur through a direct examination that would prove, once and for all, that microbreweries were incompatible with Hermosa Beach.

TMWSHH: *You mentioned a brewery up north called Anchor. How long has that brewery been there?*

Buddy: *Since 1896.*

TMWSHH: *So I'm going to assume that in 1896 there was probably not a whole lot around that neighborhood.*

Buddy: *I don't know. It was San Francisco. The Gold Rush.* The city manager, who was originally from Northern California, felt compelled to weigh in. To this point he had been just a bystander to the legislative conga line.

City Manager: *Potrero Hill in San Francisco? Probably almost as dense then as it is now. Except it was probably made out of canvas* [in 1896].

In fact, the 1890 census shows San Francisco had a population of approximately 300,000 and was larger than Washington DC, New Orleans, or Detroit. It was easily the largest city on the West Coast. Potrero Hill was close to the center of it.

The Man Who Shakes His Head dismounted Buddy's leg like an angry hound, unsatisfied.

~

In politics, preparation will always help you. Whether it's debate prep with your team or knowing your issues back to front, taking the time to research and consider the facts beforehand will always serve your interests.

The same is true of knowing your opponent. Know your opponent's issues so you can draw him or her away from them. Know their alliances, so you can know what stances they've tied themselves to. And know their performance strengths. Is he or she a good orator? Is he or she prepared at meetings? Does he or she think on their feet or need notecards at every turn?

Buddy was able to spoil my colleagues' attacks with facts and passion. He had done his research, and he knew his opponents.

For your campaign, you should do the same.

~

Eventually city council member Boyd Goodfellow had the opportunity to speak. He asked the planning director about the other uses permitted in the industrial park.

The planning director confirmed that if Buddy wanted to start a business mixing petroleum for motorboat fuel in the exact same building, our zoning code expressly allowed him to do it. No approval from the city council, planning commission, or Anti-Oil Evangelica was necessary.

But mixing barley, hops, yeast, and water was not allowed.

Some People Don't Like the Smell of Grape-Nuts

Buddy's experience was the quintessential example of an anti-business city council. It was also an unfortunate example of the power some gadflies wield in the process.

While I was on city council, we frequently regulated the number, size, and placement of televisions in restaurants. According to my colleagues (and Anti-Oil Evangelica and Beecher), a fifty-inch television encouraged less drinking by patrons than say, a seventy-five-inch one would.

Like the residents of the stodgy town in the movie *Footloose*, my colleagues toyed with the idea of banning dancing in bars. I once watched Gurney Frinks and Cliff Clouseau attempt to redesign the size and placement of rooms in an expensive boutique hotel because a neighbor (yes, *one* neighbor!) questioned the hotel's proposed parking configuration. These are people who never held jobs in private industry, much less knew the first thing about running a restaurant, engineering parking configurations, or designing a hotel. My experience on the city council taught me that government doesn't create anything; it only makes creating things of value either more or less difficult.

In Hermosa Beach, we were usually in the more-difficulty business.

Nine Secrets for Getting Elected

∽

So, what happened to Buddy and his dream of opening a microbrewery in Hermosa Beach?

Not surprisingly, after his experience with my city council colleagues and the Pit of Administrative Despair, Buddy never applied to open a microbrewery in Hermosa Beach. Instead, he opened it in neighboring Torrance and called his business The Dude's Brewing Company, after Jeff Bridges' character in the movie *The Big Lebowski*. Bumper stickers bearing quotes from the movie adorn the brewery's glistening white tile walls (*The Dude Abides*), and the Hermosa Beach Pier at sunset is prominent as the company's logo.

In September 2014 I attended the opening of the tasting room at The Dude's Brewing Company in Torrance. The brewery's new tasting room was in a space in front of the vats and kettles and canning lines. The 15,000-square-foot brewery had a maximum capacity of 60,000 barrels annually, roughly 25,000 less than Anchor in San Francisco, but as the plant got up to speed it was producing roughly 2,500 per year. The brewery already employed seven people full-time and expected to increase that number as it ramped up production.

Demand for their brew was growing, and they already supplied local restaurants and high-end specialty grocery stores like Gelson's and Whole Foods. The Dude's Brewing Company is on track to become one of the largest craft beers in the region.

While I was tasting the South Bay Session Ale (it is delicious), I asked one of Buddy's business partners if they had run into the same problems in Torrance that they did in my city.

Secret No. 5 – Be Prepared for the Ridiculousness

No, none, was the answer. *Torrance wanted our business. It seemed like the inspector's main concern was getting back after we opened to taste our beer!*

Hermosa Beach could have been home to The Dude's Brewing Company. Instead, we lost the business, revenue, and jobs to a neighboring city because three members of the city council were worried about angry phone calls and e-mails from one constituent.

Turns out, some people just don't like the smell of Grape-Nuts.

SECRET No. 6
Be Principled (Even When It Hurts)

It All Started So Well . . .

The August 12, 2013, city council meeting started well. In fact, the first forty-five minutes of it were among the best I'd had during my time on city council.

I was serving my second term as mayor, and I began the meeting, as I did every meeting, by recognizing champions in our community.

I would usually start our meetings from my seat in the center of the council dais and would then move to the chamber floor to present a proclamation to whomever it was we were recognizing that evening.

But on August 12th, I called the meeting to order from the chamber floor. The young airman in the immaculate, dark-blue service dress uniform and the two linebacker-sized men sitting in the front row were the reason why.

The young enlisted man standing at attention beside me was the Outstanding Airman of the Year at the nearby Los Angeles Air Force Base. As a former Air Force officer, I was already beaming at the opportunity to recognize someone from my branch of the armed services, but this young man made me proud in a way I can barely describe.

Originally from Kenya, the airman had won entry into the US through the immigration lottery; he was one of fifty thousand people selected at random from everyone worldwide who applied for a green card that year.

When I presented him with a proclamation from the city, I asked him what spurred his decision to enlist in the Air Force. The airman answered, *I wanted to do something to repay the country that saved my life.*

When the crowd finished applauding, I turned my attention to the two men sitting in the front row, Jarret Stoll and Matt Greene.

Everyone in the room knew Stoll and Greene. They were professional hockey players with the Los Angeles Kings, and they had just won the Stanley Cup. Both Stoll and Greene were Hermosa Beach residents.

I presented the two hockey players and the Kings' CEO with awards for their championship season and thanked their organization for being such generous partners with Hermosa Beach.

The Kings organization was delighted by the recognition, too, and actually produced a short video about the meeting that night, which they posted on the team's website. The video also ran as a special on Fox Sports West.

Remember how I said the meeting got off to a good start? It did. But the feel-good atmosphere in the room lasted about as long as a wisp of thirdhand smoke.

The signal to spring the ambush was a letter.

At the time, Hermosa Beach's city manager was in the process of looking for a new police chief and had narrowed the field of candidates to two. On July 26, 2013, for reasons I'll get to in a moment, I issued a press release endorsing one of the two finalists. This was unusual, perhaps even unprecedented in Hermosa Beach, because mayors and individual council members typically didn't deal independently with the press.

But this was an unusual situation that demanded action, and I decided to make my preference known (more on that in a moment, too).

A former Hermosa Beach city council member who held sway with a faction of the city council—let's call him Karl—came to the microphone to critique my press release.

He stole the show with malicious ease.

By the time Karl spoke, the question of the selection of the police chief was moot because the city manager had already made his choice a few days before. He'd selected the *other* candidate, the one I had not endorsed. My press release and stated preference had no effect on the process or the city's manager's ultimate decision.

But that wasn't why Karl wanted to address the city council.

Karl told the council and the public watching at home that my press release was a thinly veiled attempt to undermine the city manager's authority.

I think that action both undermines the city manager and the new chief of police, Karl said, *and it muddies the line of command.*

According to Karl I had displayed overt intent to disrupt the established procedure and protocol, and he urged the others on the council to take action and stamp out whatever embers remained from my stillborn coup d'etat.

Secret No. 6 – Be Principled (Even When It Hurts)

I was in the middle of a political knife fight before I realized it had begun.

⌒

In politics, people will repeat the trope that you must expect the unexpected. I've always thought that saying was a bit too pat, as if there were a way to account for every possibility and still lead a functional life—but there is some truth to it. I don't think there's any real way to prepare, but you should know that at some point in your political career, you will find yourself in the path of a bomb falling from a clear blue sky. Something, somehow, will go terribly wrong. And unless you are incredibly lucky, you probably won't see it coming.

The best tool to cope with it will be to take a deep breath, make it a point not to overreact, and stick to your values. Go back to basics—what do you believe in? What do want to accomplish? What have you been elected to do? Keeping your principles foremost in your mind will help you survive the explosion.

. . . And Then Things Went South

Mr. Mayor, Cliff Clouseau said as soon as I'd finished the recognition ceremony with the two Los Angeles Kings and the young airman, *I want to speak to [Karl's] letter.*

His voice quavering ever so slightly, Clouseau read from a prepared statement expressing his displeasure with the press release, citing it as one more example of my *disruptive or even destructive behavior* while in office. When he'd finished, Clouseau demanded I confess my sins against the city.

The well-coordinated political bushwhacking had begun.

Following in sequence like dive-bombers, Gurney Frinks

and The Man Who Shakes His Head swooped in to deliver their blows.

Gurney Frinks, who had also prepared for this moment, read from his own prepared statement and demanded that I *cease and desist this unprofessional behavior, because frankly, I'm sick of it.*

TMWSHH, momentarily channeling the very worst of George W., spoke third and said *ethics [had been] broken* by my press release.

They all said they wanted a public apology, and they wanted one for the city manager as well. They knew I wasn't going to give them what they wanted, and as it turns out, *that* was exactly what they wanted.

∽

I normally enjoyed counting coup with Cliff Clouseau. He was not good on his feet, and this forced him to write out whatever he planned to say in advance of debates. But like a comedian who reads his jokes from the page, Cliff Clouseau was in trouble as soon as he exhausted his prepared material or the debate took an unanticipated turn. This added to his already dour, headmaster-like demeanor made him ineffective: I once sat next to him at a candidates' forum and saw the top notecard of the many he brought contained a one word reminder—SMILE. Gurney Frinks and TMWSHH likewise tended to shy away from engaging publicly, and for the same reason—the cut-and-thrust of debate wasn't their forte, either.

When Cliff Clouseau sallied forth to engage, it was easy to flank him because he was only capable of arguing from a fixed

Secret No. 6 – Be Principled (Even When It Hurts)

position. When it started, I expected this attack would be no different. And because I was focused on my three colleagues on the dais, I didn't see that the mastermind of the ambush was the man standing before me at the podium—Karl.

Just as I had watched my colleagues and knew their reactions and tendencies, so he had watched me and knew mine. Karl knew how I would react. And because I was looking the other way I was blindsided by what happened next.

⌇

Not only did I refuse to apologize to my colleagues, but I also scolded them for spending our precious city council meeting time on a moot issue.

The city manager made his selection days ago, I said, *so let's not make a political mountain out of a press release molehill. Let's move on. We have other important things to do.*

I also told Clouseau, Frinks, and TMWSHH that the press release was my opinion, and that I was entitled to it regardless of what they thought. I scolded them for threatening me for what I'd said or what I believed was best for our city.

Freedom of speech may be a trite concept to the three of you, I told them, *but I take it very seriously. I wore a uniform and took an oath to defend it.*

The right to speak in dissent was protected in the first of our Constitution's amendments because it is the most fundamental to our system of government. I was exercising the freedom upon which all others ultimately depended. It wasn't a political gift, or something that could be exercised freely only with popular approval. In so many words, I told Clouseau and his political accomplices what they could do with their request for an apology. And the horse they rode in on.

My opponents were unmoved. Worse yet, Karl must have anticipated my full-throated defense, because when I finished, Clouseau shuffled through his papers and produced a second prepared statement. He announced that my press release was *an inappropriate action*. He charged that I had *willfully and recklessly publish[ed] a press release* that *endorse[d] one candidate and disparage[d] another*. When he'd finished reading his political indictment, Clouseau asked my colleagues to censure me.

Those few moments it took Cliff Clouseau to read his list of crimes and misdemeanors were the most excruciating moments I ever had on city council. There was nothing I could do. There was nowhere to go. I wasn't even exactly sure what a "censure" motion was, or what the consequences of it would be, but it didn't sound good. Whatever it was, there were three votes to do it sitting to my right and left.

I also remember thinking while Cliff Clouseau spoke that my colleagues were going to try to punish me for something I had *said*. I hadn't *done* anything. I had been raised to believe that apart from yelling *FIRE!* in a crowded theater, I could say damn-near anything I wanted. Doubly so if what I wanted to say was political.

Maybe so, but according to Cliff Clouseau, Gurney Frinks, TMWSHH, and their handler, Karl, those rights didn't apply to opinions about a prospective police chief. My rivals were going to use their political power to punish me for voicing a dissenting opinion.

Maybe the worst part of all was that whenever Clouseau

used the word *censure*, in my head I kept hearing the word *impeachment*.

My God, I thought, o*n top of everything else, these three are going to turn me into Bill Clinton!*

Oily Roots

Like everything else that was going on in Hermosa Beach in late 2013, this was ultimately about—you guessed it—*oil*. You'll read more about this in the coming chapters.

Karl, another anti-oil evangelical, had opposed oil drilling in Hermosa Beach all the way back to the 1980s. Unlike the younger anti-oil zealots, Karl was politically astute, clever, and not prone to apocalyptic rhetoric. He did not exude the simmering rage of Hermosa John Brown (you'll meet him soon) or paroxysmal mania that possessed Cohn the Younger (you'll meet him too). Karl was exactly the opposite. Like Brutus at the Forum, he referred to me as his *friend and colleague*, and spoke penitently about how it hurt him to have to criticize my actions in public. It would have been completely consistent with the tone of Karl's comments that night if he had shown up in a toga and paraphrased Shakespeare's famous line: *It was not that I loved the mayor less, but that I loved Hermosa Beach more!* Karl was even more dangerous than Brutus because he was patient, indirect, and able to manipulate others into wielding the knife.

In politics, some allegations of misconduct, accurate or not, are just as damning as the misconduct itself. Karl and my opponents had begun the political alchemy of turning a press release into an act of sedition. Karl knew the most important result of this would be the headlines the allegations would garner: *Hermosa Beach City Council Votes to Censure Mayor Bobko.* Whether there was any misconduct to support the allegation was incidental to the charge. I had been tried and convicted when Karl masterminded the plot and Cliff Clouseau and Gurney Frinks signed on. There were exactly three angry men on my jury, and their verdict was already in. The political theater Karl had orchestrated would culminate in a final act in which the mayor of Hermosa Beach got censured. I was as much a spectator as I was a participant in this political theater.

Even if the censure process somehow got derailed, Karl knew there would be no distinction between the allegation of a political crime and commission of an actual one. The headlines would remain, and that the city council wanted to censure me for misconduct was all most people would ever know. The incriminating headlines and negative press would be almost impossible to overcome on the eve of an election, and would provide the anti-oil evangelicals with more proof that I was not trustworthy to lead the city at such a critical time.

My opponents' political mailers wrote themselves:

The mayor was censured by the city council for misconduct. Can we trust the settlement agreement he negotiated with the oil company? Do you want someone like that making choices for Hermosa Beach about its future?

Leadership Matters

I had written the offending press release because I was distressed about our police department's leadership. As is true in every city, the police chief is one of the most important local officials, because he or she is in charge of a large department that has direct contact with the public. I have worked with a number of

Secret No. 6 – Be Principled (Even When It Hurts)

exemplary chiefs, and if they are strong and capable, things go smoothly, and their departments are delightfully unnoticeable.

But if the opposite is true, the problems are painful and abundant.

I had seen these problems firsthand when I was first elected in 2006. Back then, our police department suffered from a lack of leadership.

The symptoms of poor leadership in a police department are easy to see if you know what to look for. One is an abnormal amount of union unrest. There is always some degree of labor unrest with police and firefighters, but a lack of leadership exacerbates these problems. Grievances, expensive and divisive lawsuits over promotions, harassment, and all other manner of unfair treatment will abound.

Another, more serious symptom of a leadership deficit is an increase in use-of-force and police misconduct lawsuits against a city. This is because the culture of an organization flows from the top down, and if there is no leadership setting standards and enforcing them, corners will be cut and bad institutional habits will form. For years, we had a chief who was content to spend most days behind his desk in his basement office (near the interview room!), and the midlevel officers who also happened to be the union leadership filled the vacuum.

This led to problems.

At the leadership's nadir, the union-dominated Hermosa Beach Police Department lost its public service focus. The same cadre of self-serving sergeants who led the union's bare-knuckle political activities became the department's de facto leaders. They set the organizational standards and tone in the field, and it was not long before their *Do it our way or else!* attitude permeated the entire department and began to affect the officers' interactions with the public. For a time from about 2000 through 2006 it would have been hard to distinguish the activities of the union-dominated Hermosa Beach Police Department from those of a gang. The union sergeants were running the show, and this was their city. Sounds harsh? Type "Hermosa Beach Police" into YouTube and poke around for a few minutes to see for yourself.

The lack of leadership also resulted in a spate of terrifically expensive lawsuits against the city. According to an article in a local paper, twelve separate lawsuits were filed against the Hermosa Beach Police Department (and the city) between 2004 and 2005. The facts giving rise to the suits were uniformly awful, and each claim betrayed deeper problems in the department. I got my own taste of it when those two union board members interviewed me about my candidacy back in the fall of 2005. The only thing that distinguished that interview from the POW training I got in the Air Force was the fact the union reps didn't refer to me as *capitalist invader* or a *Yankee air pirate*.

An example: In 2006, Hermosa Beach was named as a defendant in a federal civil rights lawsuit brought by the Korean American owners of a local nightclub/restaurant. The nightclub regularly hosted parties on the weekend, and our officers did not like the restaurant's African American clientele.

We don't like people like you in my town, one officer reportedly told the restaurant's owners.

It is unclear whether he meant the Korean American owners themselves or the restaurant's African American patrons. Perhaps he wasn't discriminating. Maybe he meant both.

Outright racism wasn't even the worst of it. According to

Secret No. 6 – Be Principled (Even When It Hurts)

a report in the *Los Angeles Times*, on September 20, 2003, two officers showed up to investigate a report of water pooling outside the restaurant and ticketed the restaurant's co-owner for an illegal waste discharge. A short time later they returned to arrest the man who'd identified himself as the co-owner because in the intervening hour they'd somehow determined he wasn't. This was a lot of activity over a pool of dirty water. Whether he was the owner or merely a co-owner, the man had a business that was fifty yards from the department's front door. They knew where to find him. But this had turned into something other than law enforcement.

As the young man who had identified himself as the co-owner sat in the back of the patrol car, he slumped over, unresponsive. He had suffered a seizure and bitten down on his tongue. His father, now on the scene and justifiably alarmed to see his son in a heap in the back of a patrol car, tried to assist him. He told the officers his son had a tumor that caused him to suffer seizures when his blood pressure got elevated, and that was probably what was happening. He asked the officers to call the paramedics. The Hermosa Beach fire department was also within shouting distance, and they could respond within a few minutes, if not seconds.

The police officers refused, so the man went to assist his ailing son himself.

The officers stopped him.

Instead of allowing the father to check on his son, the officer did what anyone would do when a suspect under arrest suffered a seizure from a brain tumor and was slumped, unresponsive in the back of a patrol car: he poked him in the chest and demanded he wake up. (It is unclear from reports whether he used his baton or just his hand.) The officers were so concerned about the young man's well-being that the next day his chest was bruised from their vigorous attempts to revive him.

Predictably, the charges against the young man for allowing an illegal waste discharge from a restaurant he either owned or co-owned were dropped.

A short time later the city found itself named as a defendant in a federal civil rights lawsuit. A few months after that, Hermosa Beach taxpayers coughed up $1.1 million to the young man who co-owned the restaurant.

Is the officer who thought it was appropriate to poke a man having a seizure with his baton still with our department? Of course he is. He's one of the sergeants responsible for supervising junior officers in the field. Better yet, he was one of the five members of the Hermosa Beach police union's board.

We hired a new chief of police in July 2006, and he provided the leadership that our department desperately needed. Although he and I disagreed about policy issues (for example, meter maids), there was no question that he was a real chief. He came to meetings in his neatly pressed all-black uniform with four chrome stars on his collar, something his predecessor never did. He moved his office out of the basement upstairs to where the department's main space was. He was visible in the community; he established relationships and made sure his officers did the same. People knew him and liked him. I liked him. He was a leader.

The result of all this was the disappearance of the gangster-ish *Cop Land* feel that had surrounded the union-dominated department and my city. More important, under the new chief's command, the use-of-force and misconduct lawsuits stopped almost immediately. We worked our way through the remainder of the lawsuits from the dark days, but apart from some outliers, they were becoming a thing of the past.

Management Is Not Leadership

In 2012, we hired a new city manager. Shortly thereafter, the chief decided to take over the Los Angeles department of traffic enforcement. It was a sensible decision on the chief's part. He was the old city manager's choice, and he had opportunities elsewhere. He decided to step aside and let the new city manager hire whomever he wanted to run his police department.

For the new city manager—let's call him Nick Newby—this was going to be his first and probably most important hire. It was Newby's prerogative to hire department heads, and his choices would reverberate throughout the city. Especially for the police and fire departments. If Newby put a weak or incompetent individual in charge of the police department, it wouldn't be long before we returned to the bad, old, very expensive days.

I liked Newby. I'd helped select and hire him. He and I shared similar management philosophies. He talked about strategic plans and metrics and objectives. He was "new school" in a field dominated by "old school" ideas. I liked that.

But management and leadership are different things, and it wasn't long before I was getting feedback through the ether indicating that while the former skill might have been solid, the latter was lacking. I started receiving anonymous letters from city employees about Newby. The letters were well-informed and specific. I always shared these letters with Newby at our weekly one-on-one breakfast meetings so he was aware of them. (As mayor, I met with Newby for breakfast early each week to discuss the coming week's events.) He was stung by the more personal criticism, but I encouraged him to stay the course. He was instituting changes in the organization, and there is always resistance to change, whether at city hall, in an Air Force squadron, or in the boardroom at Toyota. I told him to stick to his guns and do what he thought best, and I would support him. Newby said he understood, and tried to laugh off the criticism, but I could see he was hurt by the personal attacks from his new subordinates. As I write this, I realize that the pressure of being the new hire in the big chair probably skewed his process for finding the new police chief. Maybe it was the first time Newby had run into a headwind from within his own organization. Maybe he didn't expect this much vitriol from the laid-back folks in little ol' Hermosa Beach. Regardless, leaders need to be unflappable (or at least appear to be), and Newby was flapped. If he knew he was on the right track—and truly believed it—the opinions of an anonymous subordinate would have been of no consequence. That the criticism gave him pause made my spider-senses tingle.

Newby selected a headhunter to help him recruit a new chief. The recruiter presented him with a list of candidates, and he and the recruiter interviewed them. This took some weeks, and apart from very general updates, the process was a bit murky.

But I had to trust that the man we'd just hired to be the chief executive of a $30 million enterprise could handle it. I watched from the sidelines. The extent of my involvement in the process was a periodic inquiry at our weekly breakfast meetings about how things were going.

It's going really well, Newby told me. *I'm excited about the candidates who have applied for the position. They're all real high-quality folks.*

With the recruiter's assistance, Newby eventually narrowed the field of candidates to two. When he'd made the final selection, he invited the prospective new chief to meet me at our next weekly breakfast.

I was underwhelmed. Newby's pick was nervous and stiff and tried to mask his discomfort by sprinkling stock phrases about policing throughout our discussion. I politely picked at my oatmeal as Newby's selection gave me boilerplate answers to my Hermosa Beach–specific questions. He touted his past success with community policing and extolled a belief in the "broken windows" theory Rudy Giuliani had famously used with the NYPD to clean up Times Square.

∽

When you begin a campaign (and once you're in office), you're going to want to select the best team possible. From your campaign consultants to your support staff to your volunteers, you'll want your people to be loyal, honest, committed to your cause, and (in an ideal world) smarter than you.

Embrace competence and hire ambitious people. Understand

that no one is expert in all the things you'll come across in a political campaign (or in office!), and there will be many areas in which you lack knowledge and experience. In those moments, you'll need advisors who can give you the benefit of their expertise and know-how. President Franklin Roosevelt had a group like this that he famously called the Brain Trust. You may not have a formal group like FDR did, but you should have access to people you can confide in and ask questions of. Hire the best people you can find, ask for help, and accept it when you need it. Good leaders find, hire, and develop other good leaders.

⁓

I was not seeing sparks with Newby's choice, and Newby sat there uncomfortably while I spoke with his selection, like a young man introducing his new fiancée to his mother and immediately realizing they weren't ever going to get along.

A few days after our breakfast, Newby sent the city council an e-mail stating that his candidate had abruptly withdrawn his name from further consideration. We later found out that although Newby's selection had been truthful about almost everything on his résumé, he'd forgotten one important detail: he was on administrative leave from the department where he currently worked . . . for misconduct.

We'd dodged a bullet.

But I had to ask; how did this candidate make it all the way through the screening process without anyone finding out he was under investigation for misconduct? How was the recruiter unaware that her client was under investigation when she referred him to us? And even if the recruiter did not disclose this information to Newby, surely someone on our end made a call to the applicant's current employer and asked questions, right? This was the basic background checking any employer would do prior to hiring an executive, and we didn't.

These oversights were a direct reflection on Newby, because he was ultimately responsible for the process. This was the kind of slow-motion bungling of a basic task that calls core competency into question, like finding a dirty bathroom in a restaurant. If they can't keep something as basic as the commode clean, isn't it reasonable to wonder what the kitchen looks like?

Newby and I had breakfast shortly after this fiasco to discuss what had happened. After laying blame for the misfire on the deceitful applicant, he told me he was thinking about hiring one of the other candidates he'd passed over during the initial search. He inquired about his second-choice candidate and learned he had already taken another position. Newby was contemplating hiring the third-place candidate. He asked what I thought.

I told Newby I was relieved we didn't make a bad hire. I also told him the process was important, and I didn't have a whole lot of confidence given what just transpired. I asked if he was sure about this recruiter.

Oh yes, he said, *she's fine. This result was a one-off,* he assured me, *an anomaly that wouldn't happen again.*

I remained skeptical. More than that, I was dismayed that Newby essentially blamed the counterfeit cop instead of assuming responsibility for the mishandled recruitment himself. He was the city's chief executive after all, and responsibility for the process was entirely his. Newby mouthed some of the right words about his responsibility for what had occurred etcetera etcetera, but there was always a qualifier. Effective leaders avoid excuses. Nobody else gets blamed. They instead take honest measure of where they've fallen short, adjust for windage, and move forward to reach the desired result. My confidence would have skyrocketed had Newby accepted responsibility for the fumble. That didn't happen.

I told Newby the decision was his, but the police chief position was too important to select the third-best candidate. I told Newby that I preferred he start over from scratch. Follow John Wooden's adage, I said, *Be quick, but don't hurry*. It was more important to get the right person into the position than it was to fill the position in a hurry.

I left our breakfast that morning with my spider-senses not tingling, but throbbing. I had no confidence that Newby owned the process or accepted responsibility for the calamitous near miss. I was doubly concerned that he was willing to settle for the third choice instead of opening the process up again and accepting whatever criticism might follow. The bad old days weren't far enough in the rearview mirror for me to settle on the third-best candidate.

If Newby's first-place candidate was on administrative leave for misconduct, there was no telling what it took to finish two places lower than that.

Following our breakfast meeting and probably some reflection, Newby announced to the city council that he had decided to reboot the process. This time however, he asked some locals to help. I had suggested he do this the first time around, but the process was his and he wasn't keen on involving other people.

On the second go-round, the community's input was becoming much more important than it had been two months earlier.

I soon learned that one of the people Newby had tapped to assist him in the selection process was none other than my soon-to-be pained and regretful friend Karl.

The Arrow Missed the Apple

Sometime after Newby started the second recruitment process, a local gadfly stopped me randomly and told me how excited she was that Hermosa Beach was going to hire its first female police chief! For the gadfly, this was a significant gender breakthrough for our city.

It was wonderful news to her, but the alarm bells went off in my head like an air raid klaxon. Why did this gadfly know more about the selection process than I did?

She wasn't one of the local notables Newby had consulted for the selection. As the mayor, I should have had a bird's-eye view of everything going on in the city. Newby and I ate breakfast weekly and spoke on the phone almost daily, and the selection of a new police chief was always a topic of discussion. Yet I was learning from a gadfly who my new chief was going to be. I was already more hopeful than confident in the selection process, given the first misfire. Having a gadfly fill me in on current events didn't do anything for my faith in the eventual result.

I immediately called Newby to find out what was going on. *I don't know where she got that information*, he said. The process was still ongoing, and there were two finalists, but Newby assured me he had not made a final decision. I wanted to believe him, but the local buzz was telling a different story. I had no idea one of the finalists was female or that the other was a black man. I didn't know their names or job histories. I didn't know anything about the prospective candidates other than that there were some.

What was left of my confidence evaporated when a second person close to our police department's command staff corroborated what the gadfly had told me. It was a done deal; Newby had all but selected the female candidate as our next chief. I was told the officers in our department knew it, and the news was circulating at her other job that she would soon be taking the reins in Hermosa Beach. A lady who volunteered in the police department had more timely and accurate information about the selection process than the mayor did. I was genuinely disconcerted.

The first selection process had misfired, and from what I was hearing from my sources in the community, the second process had fired prematurely.

∽

I asked Newby for the names of the two finalists (which he was reluctant to give me), and started doing my own research—after the first misfire, I wanted to make sure someone was doing it. Over time I had developed relationships with police chiefs in Los Angeles and Orange Counties, and I planned to start calling around. The chiefs are a small fraternity, and I thought my relationships were strong enough to find out if the two finalists were good matches for my city. Like any close-knit group, nobody would say anything bad about either candidate, but I was confident the chiefs would let me know what they thought in their oblique, chief-like way. Like all references for high-level jobs, the things left out of a recommendation are sometimes more important than what is included in it.

I soon found that the candidate Newby was going to hire had most recently been demoted when the leadership at the Los Angeles Police Department changed in 2010. The reasons for her demotion were never made public. Some said it was only because the new chief of the LAPD wanted his own people in the top spots.

Newby was quick to adopt this view. *Her mentor departed and the new guy wanted his own guy in the job,* he told me. *Nothing strange about that.*

Maybe, but it's my experience that stellar performers aren't typically demoted, regardless of what happens at the top of the organization. This is as true in a law firm as it is in a fighter squadron. It was troubling that Newby was so quick to dismiss the demotion as garden-variety political housecleaning, especially since he had no better information about it than I did. Some of the people familiar with the inner workings of the LAPD suggested that the step-down signified something more, although nobody behind the Blue Wall would say exactly what.

Whatever Newby lacked in leadership ability, he more than made up for in political savvy, and he knew he didn't need to open the process to me to show me his was the best choice. This was especially true because there was more than anecdotal evidence to suggest otherwise. Apart from discussions about her gender and an explanation for her recent demotion, I never heard much about the new chief. I certainly never heard any candid discussion about her operational or command experience. As I reflect on it, I understand now that those things weren't discussed because none of them mattered. Newby had done the political calculus, and for someone who had already publicly struck out once, this was the safe thing to do. And who could possibly oppose the selection? I could see Newby triangulating between a city council majority, a faction of political correctness enforcers in the community, and the press. Newby was making what he saw as a politically bulletproof choice.

A short time later the names of the two candidates found their way into the local papers.

Shortly after that, I started getting anonymous e-mails.

"A Full-Scale Internal Affairs Arachnicide Investigation"

The first e-mail I got came from an anonymous account. The e-mail had attached to it an article from the October 23, 1999, *New Times*.[7]

There was nothing else in the e-mail, no caustic warning or screed against the city's prospective new chief. (Although I got those, too.) In fact, apart from the PDF copy of the fifteen-year old article, there was nothing in the body of the e-mail at all.

But the article, titled "Spidergate," was a scathing report about an investigation our new chief conducted at one of her prior postings with the Metropolitan Transit Authority (MTA). The title of the article was a reference to the subject of the inquiry, an incident involving the killing of a black widow spider some of the MTA officers kept as a "pet."

In the author's words, *It was hard to believe that such a bizarre*

---

[7] Jan Golub, "Spidergate" *New Times*, Vol. 2, No. 43 (Oct. 23-29, 1997).

story could be true. . . . Some transit cops, it seems, were keeping a black widow spider as a pet in a dry aquarium. The spider, named Janice, after an African American policewoman, turned up dead [which led to the chief ordering] a full-scale Internal Affairs arachnicide investigation.

As ridiculous as this sounds, it wasn't even the worst part.

Again, the author's words: *Spidergate wasn't just about a Windexed bug, any more than Watergate was about a two-bit burglary. . . . It involved a Byzantine web of investigations, sexual harassment and otherwise, suspensions, firings, arbitrations, and lawsuits concerning complaints, many of them more petty than arachnicide. It was about [the Chief], whose departmental disciplines had ruined careers and even some people's lives.*

Maybe the *New Times* had it in for our new chief-to-be. But it's hard to imagine a mainstream publication harboring some sort of vendetta against an otherwise obscure MTA police chief. The article's author appeared legit, and a Google search of his name showed he subsequently wrote for other publications like Salon.com and the *LA Weekly*. He was experienced in police and police culture, and specialized in watchdog reporting about both.

Assuming this was a legitimate piece of investigative reporting—and there was no reason to believe otherwise—the sadly comical events described were more than enough to make any prospective employer think twice about hiring this person.

⁘

I wasn't sure what to do with the article. In fact, I'm no more sure today what I should have done with the article than I was when I received it.

I circulated the article to a few close friends and asked, assuming the allegations in the story were valid, if they would hire the article's subject at their businesses. The uniform response: No.

I thought about what to do. There were really only two choices: publicize the article or do nothing.

I felt compelled to do something because I had doubts about the integrity of Newby's process, and I was almost certain his background check would miss this, intentionally or not.

On the other hand, the politician in me knew that publicizing the article would be shouting at the wind because Newby had already done his political calculations and made a decision. He was not going to be swayed by the article, just like he wasn't going to be swayed by the demotion or the slew of anonymous e-mails I have to assume he was also getting. None of this or anything else was going to deter him.

In retrospect, the safest political path would have been to accept that Newby was going to make his choice and move on to the next thing. But this was important, and I was genuinely concerned that we would revert to the bad ol' days if we did not have the best possible leader for our department. I had deep doubts about Newby's decision-making process and the particular faction of Hermosa Beach he was playing to, so I did what every minority member of a public body does in the similar situation—I decided to speak out.

On July 26, 2013, I issued a press release to the *Los Angeles Times* and the local papers endorsing the other candidate for the chief's position.

"I had the privilege of interviewing the final two candidates," I wrote, "and I will be offering the City Manager my personal support for [the other candidate's] appointment. His reputation among leaders in the law enforcement community is sterling, and his qualifications are impeccable."

I wanted Newby and the politically correct viziers like Karl who were whispering in his ear to defend their choice on the merits, and this was the only way I knew to make them do that. If their selection was truly the best choice, it should have taken Newby (and Karl) no time to explain why. All they had to do was tell the public that their selection had the command experience, operational know-how, and leadership credentials our department needed.

That defense never came.

Instead, Newby, Karl, and their abettors on the city council turned on me. That they took such offense at an opinion that differed from theirs confirmed my fears about the integrity of the process.

To paraphrase the Bard, methinks they doth protest too much about an objection to selecting the lady.

At our next breakfast meeting, over our bowls of oatmeal, my constructive relationship with Newby ended. Newby told me how disappointed he was that I had publicly endorsed the other candidate. He used the word *disappointed*, but he was obviously angry. The new city manager didn't like the attention my press release was drawing to his decision and would have preferred to fast-forward past the vetting part of the process right to the public approbation part.

Based on what I'd seen, I told Newby that he'd made a politically motivated selection, and that it was too important for me to let pass without objection.

You're entitled to do whatever you think is best, I said, *but I'm entitled to comment when I think you're making a mistake.*

I was especially likely to object when I believed, as I did now, that he was playing politics. *If the same information about your choice for police chief had come out about you during the hiring process,* I told him, *you wouldn't be sitting here now.*

Four days after my press release, Newby made public the selection I'd heard about almost a month prior from the gadfly. Hermosa Beach officially had its first female police chief.

As soon as the selection was public, the press called me for comment. I had expected this and resolved to close ranks behind Newby's choice. I was not going to be the cause of dissension, and I wasn't going to do anything to undermine the new chief's ability to lead her department. I wasn't going to do anything to make her task any harder than it was already going to be, and I wanted everyone to know I wouldn't. In a public act of conciliation, I administered the oath of office to the new chief at her induction ceremony, with the police chiefs from all the neighboring cities in attendance. The press was there. A photograph of the two of us standing eye-to-eye, palms facing, was the cover of the local paper. And that, I thought, was the end of it.

I was wrong.

∽

There was a scene in the first season of *Game of Thrones* in which the queen of Westeros, Cersei Lannister, issues a warning to her political rival, Ned Stark. *In the game of politics*, she tells him, *you win or you die.* The ruthless queen was right. A short time later Ned Stark lost a political chess match with the queen and then he lost his head. Had he maneuvered more ruthlessly in the political arena, it's likely he might have kept it. But as everyone who watches the show knows, the queen's mercilessness prevailed, and Ned Stark's honorable head ended up in a basket.

Some of my more aggressive advisors thought I needed to act like Queen Cersei, lest I end up like Ned Stark. *Blow the whole thing up,* they said. *Take a page from your opponents' playbook and track down the "Spidergate" article's author and invite him to come talk about what he wrote at our next council meeting. Choreograph a line of witnesses to publicly air their grievances about the new chief and what she did to them at the MTA. The press will have a field day. Make Newby refute the allegations live, on TV. Be ruthless,* they advised, *because you've already seen that your opponents will be ruthless with you.*

The collateral damage from this path would have been lasting and substantial. The prospective chief's career would probably have ended in a hail of acrimony, stories about Windexed spiders, and claims of sexual harassment. These types of situations tend to gather steam on their own, and no other prospective employers would invite the unwanted attention the prospective new chief would generate. Politicians are funny like that. Nobody would want a reprise in their city of the political drama that would have played out in the Hermosa Beach City Council chambers.

It would have also put the proverbial albatross around Newby's neck. Another muffed selection process less than a year into his tenure would have called his abilities into question. And rightly so. There would have been irresistible pressure to fire up the recruitment machine a third time. A fourth recruitment process would probably have been an even-money bet too—for a new city manager.

I chose the Ned Stark approach and didn't do any of these things. I had confidence that vigorous debate sharpened issues and always led to a better decision. If you can't defend your position, you might want to rethink it. My political opponents had no such reservations and saw this situation as Queen Cersei did—*You win or you die*. There was nothing in between. For Cliff Clouseau, Gurney Frinks, and Karl, the *ad hominem* attacks and diversionary tactics were an attempt to paper over their inability to respond meaningfully to criticism.

Within days, the papers took my press release, but instead of writing about a history of spurious sexual harassment claims and mismanagement by the person we were about to put in charge of our police department, reporters were writing headlines about "censure" and my disregard for the process and disrespect for "line of command."

Political Pornography

In the end, I avoided censure, but my opponents' failure to maneuver me into their political guillotine wasn't due to a lack of effort.

Following the initial ambush, my three colleagues on the city council voted to put the motion for censure on the agenda at the next meeting, which was two weeks away. Some people advised me to fight it to the end and force my accusers to make their case publicly and explain why it was a sanctionable offense for a mayor to speak out about an issue of public concern.

You're a trial lawyer, they said, *you know how to defend yourself. This is what you do. You'll have the advantage over them.*

Admittedly, fighting this cabal was my natural inclination. I knew Cliff Clouseau and Gurney Frinks were not competent debaters, and there would be ample opportunity to call out the hypocrisy of what they were doing in public.

A public showdown would also give me the opportunity to present all the information that supported my opposition to Newby's selection—i.e., the article and abortive first hire. It would be high political drama in Hermosa Beach. If I decided to fight, nobody was going to leave the room that night without a bloody nose. The debate would also probably end careers.

But it was September; there was an election less than two months away, and I knew that holding this kangaroo court would suck all the political air out of the room. To my knowledge, it would have been the first time this type of sanction was applied to a sitting city councilman in Hermosa Beach. The traditional approach to eliminate political opponents was a recall. A resolution of censure was a less complicated procedure, with the added beauty that it required only a simple majority vote from the city council and no input from the voters.

While my colleagues and I engaged in urinary combat over moot issues and thought crimes live on public-access TV, Karl and the Anti-Oil Evangelicals would point to the political fisticuffs and ask the public if these were people they trusted to solve the oil problem.

Look at them, Karl and the other anti-oil zealots would say. *Is this how you want your city leaders to act? How can we trust them to do anything important, especially about oil?*

There was no way to extricate myself from this situation cleanly, and it was precisely the type of symbolic fight I abhorred. Like the two men in Goya's famous painting, I was sunk in the political mire up to my knees with my opponents at arm's length, and for the next two months we would bludgeon each other to death. No one would win and nothing would change.

This was political pornography, pure and simple.

The worst part, from my perspective, was that regardless of the facts or my response to them, Cliff Clouseau, Gurney Frinks, and TMWSHH could write anything they wanted into their resolution of censure and there was nothing I could do about it. There was no one to whom I could appeal. There was no guarantee of due process. They had the majority of the votes. My speech would be muted. My dissent would be punished. I couldn't challenge the "facts" they included in their motion or change the language they used.

In an ill-considered moment during the initial ambush, I offered an amendment to Clouseau's censure motion that *I don't believe in the Easter Bunny*. I meant to point out the allegations' frivolousness, but my attempt at levity fell flat. My opponents seized on the comment as proof of my immaturity, ill-preparedness for office, and atrocious comedic timing. I have no doubt that if a censure motion had been drafted, the words *I don't believe in the Easter Bunny* would have been in it. Other than the *joie de guerre* of meeting my political opponents on the field, there was nothing to be gained from the fight, and there was no way for me to win it.

So, I did what my opponents originally asked me to do—I apologized. It wasn't the public act of wailing contrition Karl and his accomplices had hoped for, but it was enough to do the trick. I wrote a letter to my colleagues, which I addressed mostly to TMWSHH because I knew he was the least resolute of the three, and asked that they move past the press release and look forward to improving the city. After some calls for my head from the anti-oil zealots, two of my colleagues agreed to withdraw the motion of censure and the issue died.

Capitulating to my opponents on this is the biggest regret of my political career.

Politics is a lot like poker: Both involve putting your opponent under pressure and forcing them to make decisions. Both require a certain level of ruthlessness to be effective. For both, the consequences for being aggressive at the wrong time can be disastrous. The art of politics, as in poker, is knowing how to be aggressive enough, soon enough.

In this situation, I could have pressed my case against Newby's candidate and trumpeted my concerns about her nomination, but I knew how big a deal doing so would have been. I knew how many careers it would have affected. So I stayed quiet.

My opponents, on the other hand, chose ruthlessness, and ruthlessness won. Sadly, ruthlessness normally wins. And the question will invariably arise during your campaign (or political career) of whether you want to be ruthless. Only you can answer that question. Whatever you decide, be advised: Politics is a full-contact sport. Wear a helmet.

SECRET No. 7
Know What You Don't Know

Winning elections and governing are distinctly different skills.

Most people who seek public office already have the aptitude and talent necessary to govern. The ability to understand budgets, communicate effectively, and deal with people are things most people do in their everyday lives. The nitty-gritty parts of the job once in office are rarely discussed, and they tend to take a back seat to the sexier big-picture issues of campaigning. But whether one is running a household or a hedge fund, these basic day-to-day managerial skills are more directly transferrable from private life to public.

Political campaigning, on the other hand, is a unique skill. Like fly-fishing, playing golf, or yoga, everyone has the potential to be good at campaigning, but most people can't just wade into the middle of a Montana stream, walk onto the first tee at Pebble Beach, or unroll their mat at the local studio and be proficient without ever having held a fishing rod, driver, or pigeon pose. Practice develops skill, and practice takes time. And unlike fly-fishing, golf, or yoga, most people don't spend their weekends or vacations practicing electoral politics.

As you enter the world of politics, recognize that it is vast and as infinitely detailed and nuanced as any community. Also understand that most elections are won or lost at the margin.

This is true from Barstow to Belfast. More often than not, the gap between winning and losing will be just a handful of votes. In the 2004 Hermosa Beach city council race for example, the difference was just eleven votes.

If you're in a close race—and you will be—do everything you can to make sure those eleven votes are on your side of the ledger. A professional campaign manager can help make sure they are.

You may have campaigned on a platform of cutting unnecessary spending in the waste management sector, for example, but when you get into office, the discovery that waste haulers are your city's biggest franchisee may take you by surprise. You may be even more surprised by the reaction of certain segments of your community to proposed changes related to your city's trash and waste hauling.

You aren't expected to know everything right off the bat, but that doesn't mean you're off the hook. And just because you don't know something doesn't mean it can't hurt you.

How Much Do You Know About Your Trash?

In 2012, the City of Hermosa Beach put its contract for waste disposal out to bid. Waste collection is the largest contract in the city, and we estimated its total value to be around $15 million over a seven-year term. (Why seven years? That's how long it takes to amortize the cost of a trash truck.) For a little city like Hermosa Beach, $15 million is a lot of money, and whenever we reopened the trash contract, all the big, national waste haulers responded.

In Hermosa Beach, the selection of the city's waste hauler had historically come down to one thing: *cost*. If the city council awarded the contract to a waste hauler who cost more than the previous hauler, the city council chambers would be packed with angry residents as soon as they got their new, higher trash bills.

I said *historically* because this was how the process worked prior to 2012. But in 2012, a large, growing segment of Hermosa Beach's population believed that mitigating environmental impact, not cost, should be the primary determinant for awarding the city's trash contract.

In response to this vocal constituency, the city council commissioned a citizens' group called the Green Task Force to develop a list of priorities and environmentally friendly requirements for consideration for the new trash contract.

The one big idea to come out of the Green Task Force was that people should pay for their trash. They called the proposal "pay as you throw," and it meant each household's bill should be commensurate with the quantity of refuse put out on the curb each week. Some people in town recycled or reused everything (so-called *zero waste* households); why should they get the same bill as a neighbor who filled their rubbish bins to the brim every week? The city didn't have a one-size-fits-all approach to water, electricity, or gas bills. Why have one for trash?

Perhaps more important, *pay as you throw* incentivized people to decrease the volume of waste they generated. The less trash the city produced, the less trash went to the region's landfills, which were scheduled to close within the next few years. When they did, most Los Angeles county trash would be shipped by rail to a remote landfill in the desert—and like moving anything in volume by rail, that process was expensive. The transportation costs would be passed on to the households in our city, which would see their bills rise.

The *pay as you throw* proposal took these factors into account and hit the sweet spot of public policy where economics, common sense, and practical environmentalism converged. The Green Task Force's plan successfully aligned economic incentives for every actor in the process with socially beneficial outcomes. It was a public policy home run.

The city council adopted the Green Task Force's recommendations, and as part of the new contract we instructed the new waste hauler to make different-sized trash bins available for our residents. Each household could choose one of three different-sized receptacles; the smallest was the cheapest, the largest the most expensive.

Ah, but what about recyclables? someone asked. *We still need the blue bins for plastic, newspaper, and glass. What should we charge for those?*

Then someone else asked, *And what if people purchase the smaller container but use their recycling bin for excess garbage? How should we deal with the free-rider problem?*

No worries, said the waste hauler, who promised that the recyclables would be sorted regardless of how they were delivered to the processing plant. The waste hauler that won the contract used what they called a *single-stream* process, which meant everything that showed up to their facility was sorted at once.

During the bidding process, I toured the various waste haulers' facilities and saw how the single-stream process worked. The collected waste from the garbage trucks was emptied into the trash hauler's facility and different recyclables were blown off a huge conveyor belt by a computer-operated camera directing robotic jets of air. There was a section that puffed off plastic bottles and another where computer-guided electronic sensors identified and blew cardboard off.

The high-tech, single-stream process was dramatically better than the old-fashioned method that employed lines of people who hand-picked recyclables from a never-ending stream of trash. The waste haulers told us the process recovered more recyclables than the manual method did. And because it was more efficient, less trash would have to be shipped by rail to a landfill in a desert.

The waste haulers told us the blue bins were part of the old-fashioned process used when workers had to separate trash by hand. The bins for recyclables helped workers on the line because residents performed the first level of separation by bundling their newspapers and removing bottles and cans from other refuse. The contents of the blue bins went onto one conveyor, and the rest of the trash from the black bins went onto another. The blue bins meant less hunting-and-pecking by the manual laborers.

With the single-stream solution, residents no longer needed to worry about separating plastic, paper, and glass from their eggshells, soup cans, and coffee grounds. And there wouldn't be a free-rider problem because there wouldn't be any blue bins.

The single-stream process and the new contract would give Hermosa Beach residents more pricing options, and the results would be more effective at preserving the environment.

Economically and environmentally, everyone was a winner. Well, not so fast.

The Big E

Hermosa means beautiful in Spanish, and for the people in Hermosa Beach the word *environment* means our beautiful beach and ocean. Broadly speaking, everyone who lives in Hermosa Beach, regardless of political stripe, is here for some combination of the same reasons: surf, sunshine, and sand.

But as I got into local politics I soon learned a growing number of people in Hermosa Beach and Southern California believed that another environment was even more important than a clean beach and pollution-free ocean: The Big-E environment.

The Big-E environment is the one Al Gore famously identified in his movie *An Inconvenient Truth*, and it embodies more than the 1.4 square miles of Hermosa Beach. It's bigger than Los Angeles, or even the state of California.

The Big-E environment includes Amazonian rain forests and the Great Barrier Reef in Australia. It encompasses oil drilling off the Malaysian coast and pollution in the Ganges. These problems are important and interconnected, and the common denominator for all of them is the excess consumption and exploitation of Earth's resources. Sadly, according to Mr. Gore and his Big-E environmental disciples, the United States is the primary culprit responsible for the spoliation.

The growing flock of Gore's disciples, many of them people who lived in places like Hermosa Beach, heard the message and wanted to do their part. And although they might not be able to save dolphins from barbarous Japanese fishermen, they could save the delta smelt (an endangered species of small fish) in the wetlands north of San Francisco. And if they couldn't do that, they could save old growth trees from being cut down in the Hollywood Hills, or institute Meatless Mondays at their kids' schools.

Wait, you've never heard of Meatless Mondays?

In 2006, the same year as Mr. Gore's movie, the United Nations identified cattle as the greatest threat to the planet's climate, wildlife, and forests. According to the UN report, cattle and livestock are responsible for generating more greenhouse gases (the ones that cause global warming) than cars, planes, and all other forms of transportation put together. The people who consume beef perpetuate this ruinous practice, and their high-protein Western diets are responsible for the acceleration of global warming. In fact, in 2016 the California Assembly passed a bill regulating greenhouse gasses produced by cattle and other farm animals.

The governor and the members of our assembly believe that California's cows have their hoofprints all over the global warming problem because they produce environment-killing amounts of methane when they belch, pass gas, and make manure.

Accordingly, preserving the Big-E environment requires that we wean ourselves from the environmental evil of cheeseburgers and barbecue. Hence, Meatless Mondays in public schools.

Although Meatless Mondays, preservation of old-growth trees, and saving the delta smelt are important, that doesn't mean the deepest green California Democrats have abandoned their traditional party canons about the primacy of public employee unions, a woman's right to choose, or gun control. They haven't. But it's hard to get overworked, wealthy Hermosa Beach residents to show up for a rally supporting minority voting rights.

It is entirely possible, however, to turn out a thousand people on a Saturday morning to hold hands on Hermosa Beach in symbolic opposition to oil drilling.

It is no exaggeration to say that while Democrats in Fresno are worried about unemployment, failing schools, and spiking crime rates in their communities, their party brothers and sisters in Hermosa Beach are more concerned about delta smelt and polar bears.

By the end of my tenure on the city council in 2013, the Big-E environment had risen in importance to the point that it received equal billing with the city's nuts-and-bolts services, including public safety.

An example: Hermosa Beach's most prominent Big-E environmentalist and Self-Appointed Guardian of the Earth (SAGE), was a shaggy-haired, '70s-era hippie who owned a multimillion-dollar three-story home two blocks from the beach. The SAGE was prominent in local Democratic politics and an influential member of the increasingly liberal Beach Cities Democratic Club. In a state known as the breeding ground for liberal Democrats, the Beach Cities Democratic Club were capital-L, Berkeley-grade liberals. In 2006, the club had become so virulently left-wing they refused to endorse six-term incumbent Congresswoman Jane Harman (also the top-ranking Democrat on the House Intelligence Committee) in the Democratic primary election because she'd cast a vote in favor of sending troops to Iraq.

One particular night, the SAGE was upset with a line item in the city budget for the police department to purchase a conventional, combustion-engine police car. The police needed the car for undercover investigations and naturally wanted one with a souped-up engine and special modifications.

The problem, according to the SAGE, was that a turbo-charged V-10 failed to meet even the most generous standards of environmental responsibility.

Couldn't the police use a Chevy Volt or Prius? the SAGE asked. *Battery-powered cars accelerate just as quickly as gasoline-powered ones and are quieter, too, which is good for undercover work.*

From his vantage point on a green, environmentally friendly soapbox, the SAGE couldn't see any reason for the city council to buy the police department a gas-guzzling behemoth when a nimble little electric car would do. This is the same mindset that measures the US military's effectiveness by how many gallons of oil it burns per day.

The police officers who were in attendance listened with amused disbelief. *Was this guy serious? Did he really think a Nissan Leaf was going to work for undercover police work?*

For one thing, electric cars were too small for all the gear and equipment they needed to carry, and the large batteries that powered them made the cars hard to modify.

As the officers in attendance at the meeting argued, sometimes investigations take longer than the battery's useful life, and they might have problems finding a place to plug in. The cars required hours to recharge, which would mean putting an investigation on hold while they got more juice. The extension cord was also a dead giveaway on stakeouts.

Electric cars are also conspicuous, the police told us, because some of the neighborhoods where they did undercover work were not known for having environmentally conscious cars parked on the street. A brand new Prius would stick out like a sore thumb.

But most important, in the case of an emergency like an earthquake, a situation in which there would be no available power, an electric car would be useless as soon as the battery died. A gasoline-powered car would run regardless, and could be refilled manually.

The SAGE listened to the officers' explanations, but remained thoroughly unconvinced that they were sufficient to justify the damage a turbo-charged V-10 and the fuel that monster consumed would do to the Big-E environment.

Unable to counter the officers' operational arguments, the SAGE resorted to a more fundamental challenge to their planet-hating selection: *How much undercover work do Hermosa Beach Police really do anyway?* he asked.

Thankfully reason prevailed, and the city council approved the department's purchase of the car they wanted to do their work—big, rumbling gasoline engine and all. But the SAGE's questions were telling. They revealed that there was an increasingly confident group of environmental activists who were going to measure everything—government and private sector alike—with an environmental yardstick. Their yardstick. Police work and public safety were no exception.

These types of debates became increasingly common. The Girl Scouts, who used to report on the progress of their annual cookie sales, now advocated for a citywide ban on plastic bags. Students from UCLA came to city council meetings to offer evaluations of our environmental programs and recommended things we could do to enhance them. Presumably, political activism was part and parcel of these students' course of study at UCLA, which says a lot about what Big-E environmentalism really is. (By contrast, I don't ever recall seeing political science or government majors at city council meetings.) I often wondered where students with degrees in environmental science would find jobs after graduation, other than in government.

⁓

"Hot" issues, and the cast of colorful characters who promote them, may catch you by surprise. The SAGE and his moralistic plea that we purchase electric police cars certainly surprised me, and I was a grizzled veteran of Hermosa Beach politics.

When You Don't Know What You Need to Know

The key to success is to see these things on the horizon, and the only way to do this is to work with someone whose job is to identify this stuff. In politics, as in business and in life, it's always important to know what you don't know, and political consultants often can help you do that. Hire someone who's already been through this, someone who knows the city's political history and knows where the minefields are.

Before you get started with your campaign, there are some specific things you'll need to know:

- **How many votes will you need to win?** Voter turnout can vary depending on the season. The traditional time for voting is in November, but some cities have their elections in the spring, and run-off elections are never in line with the normal voting timetable. You probably won't know how big the voter pool is until you or your consultant looks through past elections and works out the specific numbers, including the number of registered voters and their turnout history. Once you know the pool, you can figure out the baseline number of probable voters, and from there you can put together the number of votes you'll need to win the seat. That number will affect your fundraising, your budgeting, how aggressive you need to be about walking particular precincts, and the number of calls you need to make.

Some percentage of the registered voters in your district will be high-propensity voters, meaning that they turn out for every election. Target these voters first, and make sure that your issues and their concerns line up. They always vote, so you need them to vote for *you*. Find out what they care about. Your consultant should be able to steer you through the math, so don't worry too much about it now.

- **Who are the major players in your city?** Every city operates through the use of contracts with non-government associations, and these contractors can wind up being influential within a particular administration. Try to learn who they are and what they do before you get into office. Trash haulers, for instance, are big in most cities.

Some cities are home to large businesses: Skechers in Manhattan Beach, Honda in Torrance, or Disney in Anaheim. Making contact with them before you run is important too.

- **Does your city have a SAGE?** A SAGE is a local historian, influencer, or community activist. You'll want to forge relationships with them because they can be incredible sources of information. Sometimes known as "the Chattering Class" thanks to their fondness for talking amongst themselves, they know the city's political history, they know what the candidates are doing, and they know everyone's background. Take them out for coffee. Ask their opinions on the issues currently facing the city, and you'll get back a knowledgeable, in-depth answer that can inform your own positions.

As you'll soon see, had I asked someone involved in our schools what they thought of the blue bins issue, they might have shrugged off the question. Whereas if I had asked a *parent* if they were okay with us getting rid of the blue bins, their opposition to the proposal would have been immediate and forceful. I could have accounted for their concerns and adjusted my position to accommodate it.

One of the most useful things you can do on the campaign trail is sit and talk amicably with people who know the lay of the land. I used to have a list of people in Hermosa Beach whom I would make a point of calling every week or so, just to find out if there was anything bubbling up in their sector of the community.

Reporters are another good source of information, so if you're friendly with the local reporters, lob them a call every now and again. You need to be able to take the pulse of your community, and talking to these sages is the quickest, simplest way to do that.

Hollow Symbolism

In September 2012, the city council decided to ban polystyrene. You might know it better as Styrofoam. You are probably only aware of it when you take food out of a restaurant, and this, of course, was exactly what the ban was aimed at.

Not wanting to pick a fight with the deep pockets and tax revenue generated by big grocery stores, the Big-E environmentalists carved out exceptions in their ban for polystyrene used to package raw meat, fish, and dairy products. More people buy raw chicken or a gallon of milk contained in plastic each week than get takeout from the local restaurants, but that was beside the point. It was much safer to take a symbolic stand by directing the ban at the city's small restaurants than it was to pick a fight with well-funded corporate grocery stores like Vons or Ralph's. The local hole-in-the-wall restaurant wasn't going to challenge the ban, because paying lawyers would cost more than just buying new paper takeout containers. The corporate grocery stores on the other hand, would resist.

But effectiveness was a footnote, because the Big-E environmentalists would be able to claim a leadership role in protecting the city, complete with the self-congratulatory press releases and

Secret No. 7 – Know What You Don't Know

speechifying. Never mind that the ban did not make taking polystyrene onto the beach illegal, or that the largest source of the material was still being used in bulk by our grocery stores. Hermosa Beach was taking a stand, and that's what was important.

The symbolic stand the Big-E environmentalists took, however, had real-life consequences for Hermosa Beach's small businesses. As sympathetic as the local business owners were to the small-e environment, they told us the alternatives to polystyrene for packaging food were not good, and that their customers complained. A paper container full of leftover pad thai from the local Thai place was soggy and seeping onto the back seat before it got home. It disintegrated into a puddle in the refrigerator by morning. A local fruit smoothie shop said it was losing customers to neighboring cities because they were forced to use paper cups that leaked in people's cars.

The ban, while symbolic to the Big-E environmentalists, was costing local small businesses real money.

Perhaps the worst part of the ban was that nobody without a degree in chemical engineering could be sure what it was we had outlawed. Here's the first sentence of what we made illegal in Hermosa Beach: *thermoplastic petrochemical material utilizing the styrene monomer including but not limited to polystyrene foam or expanded polystyrene processed by any number of techniques, including but not limited to fusion of polystyrene spheres, expandable bead polystyrene, injection molding, foam molding, extrusion blow molding, extruded foam polystyrene and clear or solid polystyrene.*

A gold star for you and your high school chemistry teacher

if you can distinguish *expandable bead polystyrene* from *extruded foam polystyrene.*

⌒

A good political consultant will tell you to watch out for the impulse to ban something that people complain about.

Bans are hard to enforce, and once the enthusiasm for symbolically ridding your town of secondhand smoke or plastic bags wears off, the reality of it can quickly become ridiculous. Giving in to the clamor can feel like you're accomplishing something, but don't vote for things you don't believe in just because a vocal group bays for it at your council meeting. Your voting history will follow you from position to position. Remember why you're running in the first place. Are you running just to win a title? Or are you running to make your community a better place? If you want to change your city, you'll need to accept that sometimes you may find yourself on the unpopular side of an issue.

And that's okay.

⌒

Hermosa Beach is the most fertile kind of place for thoughtful, meaningful environmentalism to take root, because the residents are all small-e environmentalists. *Pay as you throw* is proof there are effective, practical solutions that don't require coercion or wasteful expenditures of taxpayer money.

Secret No. 7 – Know What You Don't Know

As columnist Peggy Noonan wrote, "Explaining what you believe involves trusting people to hear and consider; it assumes they will respond fairly and even with their highest selves. In this way, you develop a relationship with people, an ongoing conversation between your articulations and their private thoughts."[8]

During my time on the city council, communication with the public was almost always done *post hoc*. A conversation between the government and the public requires both sides to have something meaningful to say. But in Hermosa Beach, the Big-E environmentalists rarely did.

Which brings us back to the blue bins.

The Big-E environmentalists were adamant that we needed to have them. The bins were critically important. Not because they increased the efficiency of the city's recycling efforts or reduced the amount of trash our city sent to the landfill. We needed the blue bins because they were important to the children.

What's the connection between the blue recycling bins and children? Well, for years, people have been teaching kids to separate their recyclables from other trash. In Hermosa Beach's grade school, there is a class dedicated exclusively to recycling and the environment (really).

Hermosa Beach students are taught to put their food scraps into the trash and their paper and plastic into separate recycling bins after lunch. These lessons are instilled early and often, with the idea being that children take the lessons home and incorporate them into their everyday lives.

---

8   Peggy Noonan, "Apathy in the Executive," *Wall Street Journal* (May 1, 2014).

Without the daily ritual of separating plastic bottles, newspaper, and other recyclables from the trash, we would communicate to impressionable young minds that it was acceptable to haphazardly throw things away without consideration of the Big-E environmental consequences. According to the Big-E environmentalist logic, the blue bins were symbols necessary to counter this moral decay, regardless of their actual impact on the effectiveness of recycling or the environment.

So the city council succumbed to the pressure and kept the blue bins. Each week the residents of Hermosa Beach perform the symbolic gesture of putting out two separate bins—a black one for refuse and a blue one for recyclables, even though the second bin is completely superfluous.

It would have been just as meaningful to write into the city's contract that instead of a blue bin, the waste hauler must provide green balloons to each household that they could tie onto their mailbox on trash day to symbolize their commitment to the Big-E environment. The green balloons would have been just as effective as the blue bins. Cheaper, too.

SECRET No. 8
Have a Motor

What's Past Is Prologue

We sat at a table in a law firm's posh conference room in West Los Angeles, from which we could see the fairway at the Los Angeles County Country Club across a busy Santa Monica Boulevard. Hermosa Beach's management team was there. I was serving my first term as mayor.

Also present were Boyd Goodfellow (who was then mayor pro tempore), our city attorney, and our city manager. Our legal team was with us too. Our lead trial counsel was a well-respected former United States attorney with almost forty years of high-stakes trials under his belt. His name was on the firm's masthead, along with the name of the husband of one of California's two senators. A man in his sixties, our lead trial lawyer stood a lean six foot two, and he probably could still have beaten anyone in the room around a quarter-mile track. His second-in-command was a young attorney with a Harvard law degree and a love of the Los Angeles Lakers.

Our opponent, the Macpherson Oil Company, and its president, Don Macpherson (actual name), were also there. Macpherson's lawyers did not have the same pedigree ours did, but they were tenacious, and thus far they had been disturbingly effective. This was the first time I'd ever been face-to-face with the man behind the litigation that had brought my city to the brink of bankruptcy.

Coming to the meeting that morning I half expected to find Don Macpherson waiting for us wearing a black Nehru jacket and an eye patch and carrying a purring, bald Sphinx cat. What I got instead was a bespectacled guy in his sixties whom you wouldn't notice standing behind you in line at Trader Joe's.

We were all sitting around the conference room table because the trial date for our case was fast approaching and both sides wanted to take one last shot at resolving it. Leaving a case to twelve strangers on a Los Angeles County jury is always a risky proposition, and Mr. Macpherson wanted to avoid the uncertainty and expense just as much as we did.

The difference between us was that the City of Hermosa Beach had an order of magnitude more at stake than the Macpherson Oil Company did. The city's legal position had deteriorated from the start of the litigation and continued to get worse. The word *bankruptcy* had recently crept into discussions about the case because the city council had begun to evaluate its alternatives if a jury returned a verdict that was larger than we could ever hope to pay.

How did the City of Hermosa Beach find itself in this this conference room under such grim circumstances?

Oil.

The case was about drilling for oil. An accumulation of decisions by past city councils had delivered us to this fancy conference room table. As a result, we found ourselves on the eve of a bet-the-city trial that might result in Hermosa Beach simply ceasing to exist as a city.

Secret No. 8 – Have a Motor

∽

Newcomers who've won political office tend to think the only administration to watch out for is the one they've just replaced.

Not so.

Generations of past politicians have kicked problems down the road, and you will invariably have to deal with at least some of them. Odds are they will arrive on your desk even before you've unpacked your office. For example, any first-term city council member in California will be immediately confronted by his or her city's rapidly growing CalPERS obligations. These new officeholders may be shocked when their city finance departments tell them the portion of the next year's budget that will be consumed by existing obligations that were bargained for decades earlier by long-forgotten political predecessors.

Think of it like this: winning an election is a lot like showing up the morning after a house party. By the time you arrive, the people responsible for the mess are gone and there's a lot to clean up. The scope of the cleanup varies depending on your city. Some new politicians may have to tow a car blocking the driveway. Others may merely have to fish beer bottles out of the hedge. Some will have to figure out how to get gum out of the carpet.

In Hermosa Beach, the oil problem I faced was the equivalent of coming home the morning after a Bieber-level rager that had gone on for fourteen years. (Is it too late to say I'm sorry for using a Justin Bieber metaphor?)

I can understand why all those previous city councils passed on finding a real solution to our oil problem, because that would have forced them to compromise and accept a less-than-ideal reality. As I would soon learn, taking the community into less-than-ideal territory—even when reason and necessity dictate it—can make the people leading that effort *extremely* unpopular.

Know your priorities. Know what your goals in public office are. If your goal is a career in political office, you will arrive at different solutions than if your goal is to solve problems and serve the best interests of your community. Know yourself well enough to be able to tell the difference between the two.

︵

The South Bay cities along the Santa Monica Bay have a long history with oil. El Segundo, a neighboring city to the north of Hermosa Beach, is home to one of the largest oil refineries in Southern California. In fact, the name *El Segundo* means "the second" in Spanish, and the city was so named because it was the Standard Oil company's second refinery in California. For El Segundo, there was an oil refinery before there was a town.

Redondo Beach to our south had a long history with oil drilling as well, but had no active wells. Other cities in Southern California—Long Beach, Signal Hill, Torrance, and Huntington Beach—also have long histories with oil, and most still have active wells. Huntington Beach High School's football team is called the Oilers, and Beverly Hills High School (yes, the famous 90210 school) just a few miles inland has an active oil well on school property.

Like its neighbors, Hermosa Beach had an on-again, off-again relationship with oil. The city imposed a ban on drilling in 1932, which stood all the way until 1957, when Shell Oil

Secret No. 8 – Have a Motor

offered the city $500,000 to put the issue on the ballot. The voters didn't rescind the ban, but the city council kept the money and used it to build the Hermosa Beach Pier.

In the mid-1970s, the Macpherson Oil Company, then known as Windward Associates, arrived on the scene and again proposed to drill for oil. In 1984 after a long campaign to get the issue before the voters, Hermosa Beach passed measures P and Q, which allowed for limited oil drilling in the city. The voters were persuaded by the revenue the project would bring, which was needed to purchase open space and parkland, among other things. A year later the voters approved an ordinance establishing the Hermosa Beach Oil Code.

With the ban repealed, the city council signed a lease with Macpherson in 1992, allowing him to drill from the City Yard. The City Yard is approximately four blocks inland from the coastline, and the oil company proposed to tunnel underneath the city and access the oil they believed was just off the coast.

As soon as Macpherson got approval to drill, a Hermosa Beach resident who lived directly across the street from the site formed a coalition of local activists who were opposed to the project. In 1992, the project's most vociferous opponents tended to be those who lived closest to the City Yard, as was the case twenty years later.

The anti-drilling activists, who called themselves Hermosa Beach Stop Oil, sued the California State Lands Commission to invalidate the drilling approvals it granted Macpherson. Their lawsuit failed. Undeterred, the Stop Oil activists took the question back to the voters, and in 1995 the electorate approved a new oil drilling ban.

Nine Secrets for Getting Elected

The window of time in which oil drilling in Hermosa Beach was a legal activity was open for less than a decade. The problem for the city was the binding agreement it had signed with Macpherson in 1992, during the period when oil drilling was legal.

After the measure passed, the Stop Oil activists urged the city to apply the new ban to Macpherson. The city responded appropriately, stating that it would continue to perform according to the terms of the lease, because failure to do so would expose it to a significant risk of liability.

Unsatisfied with this answer, in 1997 the Stop Oil activists sued the City of Hermosa Beach to halt Macpherson's oil drilling project.

On July 23, 1998, a Los Angeles County Superior Court heard arguments from both Stop Oil and the city and decided that the new ban the voters instituted in 1995 could not be retroactively applied to Macpherson's lease. The judge found that the parties to the lease had a right to expect that the other side would do what they promised—even though the other party was a city.

Hidden like a metastasizing tumor in the judge's ruling was important language that said the city might justifiably renege on the lease if there were "real threats to the health, safety, and welfare of the community." Ruinously expensive legal battles would be fought for more than a decade to come in order to define what "health," "safety," and "welfare" actually meant, and to determine whether there were actual threats to the community.

Seizing on this language and the possible out it provided, the city council hired a consultant in January 1998 to reevaluate

Secret No. 8 – Have a Motor

the oil project's health, safety, and welfare impacts on the community. The consultant presented his conclusions to the public at a city council meeting on September 17, 1998.

By all accounts the September 17 meeting was rambunctious. The outraged and belligerent Stop Oil activists were there, along with other members of the community who opposed the project. Adding to the drama was the fact that two of five elected city council members were forced to recuse themselves from voting on the issue. One of them lived within five hundred feet of the proposed drilling site, and the other owned property close by. This left any decision about the project to the remaining three council members.

The consultant gave his presentation, which identified the risks associated with oil drilling. Opinions differed about the severity of the risks, but there was no denying that an oil-drilling project in the middle of a densely populated little beach city posed many of them. One councilman who voted that night told me that he was surprised to learn that the chance of a catastrophic event at the facility was one in seven hundred; that chance was way too significant to ignore.

I might be willing to take that chance myself, the former city councilman told me, *but I wasn't going to ask the community to take it.*

The activists heard the same statistics and beseeched the three city council members to quash the project.

Faced with a roomful of angry constituents, and given colorable concerns about the safety of the project, the city council voted that evening to terminate the lease with Macpherson.

Don Macpherson was at that meeting too. The oilman

watched a parade of activists come to the microphone and claim that he was going to ruin their city in the selfish pursuit of oil and riches. He watched the procession of accusers publicly impugn him and said nothing.

Years later we would learn how badly he felt he had been treated that night, both by the Stop Oil activists and the city council. His lasting sense of grievance motivated him to file a lawsuit, and was a significant obstacle to settlement. Events that evening, as our trial counsel would later observe, stirred some of the emotional undercurrents that swept this case toward trial.

Mr. Macpherson had seen all he needed to see that night. He knew the city's residents and its city council had turned against him and his company's project. On December 10, 1998, Don Macpherson and the Macpherson Oil Company sued Hermosa Beach for breach of contract.

We Don't Have to Make Peace with Our Friends

Avoid underestimating the ardor with which your opponents hold their views. You know what it is to care deeply about your community. You have a clear view of right and wrong. The people whose political views differ from yours (with a few exceptions) care about these things just as deeply as you do. Their passion and resolve is just as strong as yours. Maybe stronger.

By the time the Macpherson case was approaching trial I had no doubt that the litigation would eat our city head-first, so addressing the issue was my first and most important priority. If allowed to go unchecked, the problem would have a terrible impact on the lives of our residents and unthinkable long-term consequences for our city.

My colleagues and I worked hard to keep the city afloat. We made compromises where we needed to and defended our positions when we could, and ultimately we arrived at a practical solution.

In retrospect, we should have pushed further. We should have gone out into the community and explained the problem and the remedy, and what it meant we were going to have to do in the future if the case progressed to its unhappy conclusion. We should have armed our citizens with facts. We should have inoculated them against the forces that dragged everything back to what car they drove, or whether they had solar panels on their roofs, and (gasp!) whether they loved their children, because, like it or not, none of these things were going to affect our ability to deal with the bankruptcy question. We didn't get out ahead of it.

The anti-oil contingency had completely different priorities. To them, bankruptcy was a theoretical hobgoblin that would never materialize, and even if it did it would be a small price to pay to keep oil out of Hermosa Beach. Their environmentalism and anti-oil stance was unconnected to practical reality or any desire to solve problems: it was a moral obligation, and anyone who opposed them was deeply and profoundly wrong.

~

The parties involved in every high-dollar legal case almost always engage in some formal dispute resolution process. The most common process is mediation, in which both parties present their cases to a neutral third party who cajoles, persuades, and twists arms until the two sides find a compromise.

Nine Secrets for Getting Elected

The lawyers for both sides agreed that the Honorable Bill Meechum would be our mediator.[9] Judge Meechum was a recently retired bankruptcy judge in his late sixties. He was fit despite his age and had a Boston accent thicker than a pint of Guinness. Even though he probably spent more time fishing or playing golf than he did dealing with the law, the former federal judge still carried himself like someone who was accustomed to running the show.

When Judge Meechum arrived, all the lawyers and principals had already taken their places around the conference table and were doing their best to make small talk with the enemy. When the judge entered the room, the congregation sprang from their seats and assumed the friendliest possible attitude. The smiles, even from the normally stoic lawyers, were quick and wide. Everyone wanted to show the judge *they* were the reasonable ones, the truly nice people in this god-awful mess who deserved what *they* were asking for. Judge Meechum made his way around the table and shook hands with everyone. By happenstance, he reached me last.

I had not done much research on Judge Meechum prior to the mediation because our legal team was sure he was the right man for the job. The only things I knew about him were that he was a Georgetown law graduate and that he had been the federal judge who worked Orange County out of its bankruptcy in the mid-1990s.

As he made his way around the conference room that morning, I learned something else: The retired federal judge was a Naval Academy graduate. He was wearing a gold-and-blue regimental tie with the Naval Academy's crest on it. He also wore the

---

9 "Bill Meechum" is a pseudonym.

Secret No. 8 – Have a Motor

oversized, bright gold Naval Academy ring that was impossible to miss.

When he finally got to me I extended my hand. He did the same, probably happy to be done with the last of fifteen overly enthusiastic lawyers shaking his hand just a little too hard.

Your Honor, I said. *Kit Bobko, mayor of Hermosa Beach.*

Bill Meechum. Nice to meet you. He was clearly ready to end the pleasantries and get to work.

I held his hand a beat longer.

I'm a little worried because nobody told me we were going to have a squid in charge of this thing today, I said.

I wasn't looking, but I'm sure the jaws around the table dropped in unison. A sudden and intense silence enveloped the room like a fog.

Judge Meechum squeezed my hand tightly and pulled me closer to him; our noses were within eight inches of each other. His eyes narrowed. The federal judge's accent sharpened from being recognizably Boston-Irish to full-on *Bahhhst-inn Southie.*

Whey-yah did you go to school? The tone and inflection were the same as Clint Eastwood's famous question to the punk on the wrong end of his .44 Magnum.

The football school in Colorado Springs.

The Naval Academy and Air Force Academy were fierce rivals, and his alma mater had beaten mine the year prior. The games between the service academies, but especially Air Force and Navy, were always hard-fought affairs.

The slightest glimmer of a smile crept across the old Navy man's mouth. The Naval Academy and West Pointers called Air Force Academy graduates *Zoomies.* Naval Academy guys were *Squids*. The West Pointers were affectionately known as *Grunts*.

You're a Zoomie! he declared.

Yessir. Class of '91.

The judge and I both smiled.

The city's legal team collectively exhaled.

I later learned that Judge Meechum had been a fighter pilot before he took up the law. Like my father, he flew F-4 fighter jets in Vietnam. They were actually there at the same time, my father flying his missions from the air base at Da Nang, while Judge Meechum flew his missions off the *USS Ranger* from the Gulf of Tonkin.

The Georgetown law degree and his experience on the federal bench were now the second and third most important things I knew about him. A distant second and third at that.

~

Macpherson's breach of contract claim sought $750 million in lost profits and damages from Hermosa Beach. To put this in perspective, if Macpherson had asked us to purchase the Los Angeles Kings hockey team for him, we could have done that and had $300 million left over. In 2009, the city's general fund was approximately $28 million, so there was no way we could ever cover a quarter-billion-dollar judgment. Even if we escaped the trial with a judgment one tenth that size, the effects on our city would be devastating. The spectrum of probable judgments went from merely crippling (judgments we might be able to finance over many years) to death sentences that would reduce Hermosa Beach to financial rubble.

Secret No. 8 – Have a Motor

But nothing compared to the prediction we heard from the bankruptcy lawyer we brought in to prepare us for trial. A realistic assessment of the situation was that after the trial ended and the appeals were exhausted, Hermosa Beach would be broke and would probably seek bankruptcy protection from its creditors.

In 2009, the City of Vallejo in Northern California was the canary in the municipal bankruptcy coal mine. The community of 121,000 in the Bay Area was the largest California city ever to enter bankruptcy. Cities throughout the state were watching to see how Vallejo's problems would resolve. Bankruptcy presented difficult and unanswerable questions.

When an entity, business, or person enters bankruptcy it comes under the protection of federal law, and, of course, a federal bankruptcy judge comes along as part of the deal. The bankruptcy judge referees proceedings between the creditors and the debtor, and the proverbial babies are split in bankruptcy court. Creditors emerge with fractions of what they are owed, and some emerge with nothing. Debtors are reduced to zero. If Hermosa Beach entered bankruptcy it would do so under Chapter 9, which permits government entities to restructure their debts while continuing to provide essential services to the public. That sounds simple enough, but the federal constitutional issues at play were profound, and at the time, undecided.

One of the main questions had to do with the role of the bankruptcy judge and what would happen when he or she was forced to substitute his or her discretion for that of the city's elected officials. For example, we believed the city needed funding for a full complement of thirty-six police officers to maintain our public safety service levels, but that was actually a higher number of officers per capita than other similarly sized cities had. What would happen when our creditors decided, based on data from comparable cities, that only twenty police officers were required? The savings from cutting sixteen positions would free up millions that could be used to pay a judgment. Would the bankruptcy judge cut public safety to pay the city's creditors over the elected city council's objection?

Some thought a federal bankruptcy judge would be slow to impose his or her will on the elected officials, but the prevailing view ran in the other direction. Historically, federal judges had shown absolutely no aversion to superseding elected officials' authority, and this situation would be no different. I subscribed to this view. It made sense to me that if the city council voluntarily sought bankruptcy protection, we would necessarily surrender much of our authority to the court. It wasn't as though a bankruptcy judge had pulled up a chair at the city council dais. To the contrary, we had gone into his courtroom and asked for his protection from our creditors. I was certain if we entered bankruptcy that, at best, deep cuts were coming. At worst, there were going to be amputations.

The alternative to bankruptcy, and one we were forced to consider seriously, was dissolution of the municipal corporation. If the debt that resulted from an adverse judgment was more than we could bear—and the odds were that it would be—then we had to think about the possibility of our beautiful little beach city becoming a place formerly known as the City of Hermosa Beach. From our research, we believed we could disincorporate and be re-absorbed by Los Angeles County, which would assume our outstanding debts. The liability for our decision to breach the contract with Macpherson would be spread over the entire county. But even this was not a certainty, because we did not know if the Los Angeles County Board of Supervisors would be willing to take on a hundred-million-dollar judgment in exchange for acquiring a 1.4-square-mile sliver of pristine beach.

For a proud city like ours, which traced its history back to 1907, this was an unthinkable alternative. But we were now being forced to consider it.

Politics Is the Art of the Possible

At the height of our trial preparation we were burning through nearly $300,000 per month, and this did not include the time our city attorney, staff, and the city council were spending on the case.

The litigation had become our main focus. We had numerous closed-session meetings with our trial lawyers and experts to discuss strategy and get updates on the case. We had many multiple-hour-long meetings to prepare for the mediation with Judge Meechum. We walked through revenue and expenditure projections with our finance experts and discussed where we might be able to find money to fund a settlement. We talked about restructuring city functions and eliminating positions. We discussed selling city property. We were exploring every possible scenario that might make a few more dollars available for a settlement.

All of this occurred within the context of a city council that had been divided on what our negotiation position should be. Finding a true consensus among the elected officials was tough. The litigation had been ongoing for almost a decade by the time we arrived at the mediation, and many viewed it as a semipermanent state of affairs. Like a person who was allergic to antibiotics or someone who was unable to drive at night, the oil litigation was an unfortunate, chronic condition to which we had all grown accustomed.

This view was particularly true for my colleagues who had been on the council the longest. When the opportunity to mediate the case presented itself, they were willing, if only begrudgingly, to negotiate with Macpherson.

They were reluctant for different reasons. The most senior member of the city council in 2009 was Joe Kozlowski, who was in the middle of his fourth term.[10] A former Navy man, Kozlowski was an electrician who had been in Hermosa Beach almost his entire life.

Kozlowski knew the details about virtually everything that went on in Hermosa Beach. He knew what type of grass was planted in the outfield at the Little League fields. He knew what size the bulbs were in our streetlights, and how long they were expected to last. He knew what year we'd last repaired the concrete pilings on the pier. When contentious issues arose at city council meetings, I always listened to what Kozlowski had to say before I waded into the debate, because in his unique, plainspoken way, he would usually provide facts that other people simply did not know.

This little anecdote will tell you everything you need to know about Kozlowski and Hermosa Beach: Someone once told me that a resident who had purchased a multimillion-dollar

---

10 "Joe Kozlowski" is a pseudonym.

Secret No. 8 – Have a Motor

beachfront home approached Kozlowski to complain about the noise on weekends. Especially bothersome to the homeowner were the volleyball players. The new resident told Kozlowski they were hitting volleyballs in front of his new beachfront estate from sunup to dusk every day for the entire summer. Kozlowski listened, told the new resident he understood, and said he would get his hammer and come right down.

The new resident was perplexed. *A hammer?*

I'm going to help you put up the For Sale *signs in your yard,* Kozlowski told him.

Kozlowski did not believe the oil company was entitled to the king's ransom they wanted. He had followed Macpherson's progress closely through the years and thought the oil company had done little actual work toward drilling. Macpherson had applied for some of the necessary permits from the city and state agencies, but had not erected any equipment nor turned the first shovel of dirt.

Kozlowski reasoned practically: Why should the city pay the oil company for something that never appeared likely to happen? Kozlowski believed, as many in the city government did at the time, that Macpherson lacked the wherewithal to complete the project and was actually relieved by the city's decision to breach the contract because it let him off the hook.

For Kozlowski, the equitable solution was also the most obvious: pay Macpherson whatever hard costs the company had incurred right up to the point when the city decided to cancel the contract. But no more than that.

Kozlowski was universally regarded as being a reasonable and a thoroughly decent man. I think deep down he believed that if the case ever got to a jury other decent and reasonable people would see things in exactly the same way he did. There was a certain playground fairness appeal to Kozlowski's position, and I completely understood where he was coming from. Many people did. In fact, locals who want to discuss the oil case with me to this day echo his sentiments.

Dick Daley held a much more cynical view of the situation than Kozlowski. A Machiavellian through and through, the native Chicagoan saw everything through the lens of realpolitik. His political intuition and knowledge of the legal process led him to conclude the city should fight the oil company to the bitter end. There was no value in giving up before exhausting all the available legal remedies, and he knew that process would take years. Sure, the legal fees and costs were mounting, but they were a necessary evil. Whatever the magnitude of that evil, it was preferable to capitulation to the forces of darkness.

What was the downside of litigation? Daley was confident no sitting Los Angeles County judge (and he should know, he was married to one) would put Hermosa Beach into bankruptcy. If they did, what choice would we have as a city council then? The city's elected officials could point at the judge and tell the public, *The court made us do it! That bad guy or gal in the black robe did it!* If we were headed for bankruptcy, it was better from a purely political standpoint to have a judge impose the sentence than for the city council to sentence itself. Settlement was never

Secret No. 8 – Have a Motor

a realistic option for Daley, and it was absolutely no option at the price Macpherson wanted.

Daley also knew there was a vocal group of residents who would object to a payment of any amount of money to Macpherson. The larger the ransom we agreed to pay, the larger the opposing crowd would be. I knew Daley's political instincts were extraordinary, but I had not been in town when the first battle over oil had occurred, and I admittedly underestimated the depth of the anti-oil sentiment.

The third man who would be making the decision with Daley and Kozlowski had also been on the city council for many years. He would listen to the advice we got from our legal team and shake his head, which was normally the sum total of his contribution to the discussion. You've met him before in this book; he's The Man Who Shakes His Head, or TMWSHH for short. TMWSHH offered no opinions about the litigation, provided no meaningful input about the prospect of a settlement or how one might occur, and generally had very little to say that was useful regarding our predicament.

Boyd Goodfellow and I were the two youngest and newest of the city's five council members. We shared the opinion that bankruptcy was a terrible option, but we were at a loss for alternatives. The city's finances would not support a settlement in the range we knew Macpherson wanted, and that was only a fraction of the amount we might ultimately be liable for if the case went to trial. Of the five sitting council members, we were the ones most willing to negotiate with Macpherson. We were definitely in the minority.

Can You Afford to Serve?

You cannot make good decisions if you're operating on bad information. I'm not just talking about making sure your advisors are knowledgeable and trustworthy; I'm talking about making sure that you're honest with yourself. I'm talking about ridding your perspective of self-delusion.

So take a moment here, in the middle of this chapter, and ask yourself, *Can I afford to serve?*

It's not a trivial question. People tend to answer it based entirely on their financial situation, but it's bigger than that.

Politics can take a nasty toll on politicians, their families, and their friends. You might be willing to leap headfirst into the void, but are you ready to ask that of your partner? Of your children? On the weekend before Election Day in 2013, a local businessman who was a political opponent hired an airplane to fly a banner over the shoreline urging residents to "Kick Bobko and Booze Out!" of Hermosa Beach. Sadly, when it comes to emotionally charged political issues, some people can be downright awful. It's something every politician eventually has to deal with.

So before you go down this road, you need to be honest with yourself. Take a moment and think; do you really want to put your friends and family through this?

When Bankruptcy Isn't an Option

The mediation with Macpherson, like most mediations, started with the lawyers for each side presenting the highlights of their case to Judge Meechum and the other side. Following the introductions and opening statements, Judge Meechum separated

Secret No. 8 – Have a Motor

the city team from the Macpherson team and spoke to each side privately.

Our negotiation strategy was straightforward. We would offer Macpherson what we could, and if that wasn't enough, we'd resolved to take our chances at trial. If a jury awarded Macpherson more than we could pay, we'd declare bankruptcy and swallow the poison pill. Our hope was that the prospect of a difficult trial and potentially protracted bankruptcy process would encourage Macpherson to avoid the difficulty and uncertainty and accept less than he might have otherwise. We weren't interested in a trial or a drawn-out bankruptcy proceeding either, but we were backed into a corner and were running low on options.

We walked into the mediation with the bankruptcy pill between our teeth. If Macpherson pressed us into a corner, we would bite down on it like a captured Cold War spy. They wouldn't take us alive.

When Judge Meechum spoke with us privately, we explained how the city's financial status had declined over the past few years along with California's nose-diving economy. We told the judge that revenue had been flat since 2006 and our cash flow was negative. We were spending more than we took in. We explained that in the current fiscal year (2009), we were still trying to fill a $1.2 million hole in the budget. Our financial expert laid out the basis for his analysis and explained that our current finances would support no more than a fraction of the settlement Macpherson wanted. The math was the math, and those were the real, no-kidding numbers.

Or so we thought.

The old federal judge listened. He jotted down some notes. It was only a few seconds after we'd finished our presentation that our plans were in tatters on the floor.

Judge Meechum reviewed the brief we submitted outlining our position and legal defenses and told us that, in his opinion, there was a *fairly substantial risk of judgment against the city*. This was not news to us—we appreciated it in an academic sense—but somehow it became more immediate when a federal judge sitting in the same room said it. He was distressingly unimpressed by the health, safety, and welfare issues we thought were our ace in the hole. To him it was no better than a toss-up argument.

But the real damage to our plan came when he discussed the city's potential bankruptcy. Tapping a copy of the bankruptcy code he'd brought with him, Judge Meechum told us that as the main creditor, Macpherson would have to confirm any bankruptcy plan, and there was little chance of them doing that if they obtained an enormous judgment against the city.

Bankruptcy, he said, *might not even be an option for you.*

We protested. *What about Orange County? How did they manage?*

Exigency, he told us. *There was a run on the investment pool, and they were able to work out a plan to avoid a crisis. There is no exigency here. Your situation is different.*

The words struck us like a knockout punch on the point of a boxer's chin. Our knees had not buckled, but we were out; we just hadn't hit the canvas yet. The legal team, the city manager, city attorney, Boyd Goodfellow, and I all sat there. Dumbstruck. Blank.

Secret No. 8 – Have a Motor

Judge Meechum let a few moments pass and then looked at me. *So, Mr. Mayor, what else you got?*

Nothing. I had nothing else.

⸺

Macpherson's first settlement offer was in the mid-eight-figure range. Stripping out everything we could from our operations, and financing the settlement over time, we believed we could come up with a sum somewhere around $10 million. We might be able to find just a little more if Macpherson would agree to accept interest-only on the debt for the first few years of the deal.

This wasn't good enough, and Judge Meechum told us that Macpherson knew the city could do better. Just like us, the oil company had its own financial experts who had pored over the city's publicly available financial documents. Interestingly, their financial guys came to some of the same conclusions ours did. Judge Meechum told us Macpherson's team thought the city had more money stashed away than it was letting on.

Specifically, Macpherson thought we were spending disproportionately on our cops and firemen. According to what Judge Meechum told us, Macpherson's financial experts believed what we spent on public works (street repairs and infrastructure) had decreased between 2006 to 2008, but what we spent on police and fire increased by 15 percent annually over that same period. Macpherson saw that public safety represented a significant—and increasing—portion of the city's budget, even though our revenues were flat or declining over the same period. In the opinion of the oil company's financial experts, cutting overtime costs alone could enable the city to save millions, thereby making more money available for a settlement.

We learned at the mediation that Macpherson believed Hermosa Beach would save millions if we contracted with the Los Angeles County Sheriff and Fire Department for our police and firefighting services. This was heresy. The residents of Hermosa Beach were comfortable knowing we had our own public safety services. They would be unsettled if for those services they had to depend on the same agency that served the residents of Carson and Compton. But having our own police and fire departments was expensive, and the costs were rapidly running away from us.

Judge Meechum knew what would happen if we went into bankruptcy, and saw that we did not fully appreciate the repercussions. For starters, the city would end up paying hefty legal fees; we estimated about $2 million for the bankruptcy process alone, and that would have to be paid before we made any cuts. In a bankruptcy, the lawyers get paid first, and they're not cheap.

Judge Meechum also knew from years of experience that everything was going to be cut—deeply. Police and fire services were going to be first. Vallejo, for example, had been forced to cut its police force from 160 officers down to just 90 when it sought bankruptcy protection. It cut its fire department by 47 percent. Vallejo actually told its residents to use the 911 system judiciously because of the city's lack of resources. Inevitably, violent crime skyrocketed. Although he did not know the precise statistics, Judge Meechum had an intimate knowledge of the process and clearly understood the end game. He could see that we did not.

Secret No. 8 – Have a Motor

I told the former federal judge we couldn't contract with Los Angeles County. Boyd and I knew that what looked like a solution to people outside the city was a political bridge too far.

If Boyd and I go back to our city and say we're going to the county to raise money for a settlement, I told the judge, *you'll be talking to a new city council before that deal ever gets done because we'll all get recalled. This is a nonstarter. It isn't going to happen.*

Judge Meechum was not sympathetic. He listened to me, but I could see the old Irishman's face reddening. He'd heard enough. He slapped the table hard enough that the coffee mugs rattled. *Kit! We're not here for you to tell me what you're not going to do! You have to be serious about this!*

The kindly retired federal judge with the cool Boston accent had become a FREAKING-FEDERAL-JUDGE again right before our eyes. Or maybe it was a midshipman from the Naval Academy barking at a plebe. Either way, the old fighter pilot got my attention. He got everyone's attention. There were suddenly a lot of big, unblinking eyes in $600-per-hour lawyer heads all around that conference room table.

Judge Meechum had made his point: This was more serious than we appreciated, and Hermosa Beach was close to going over the edge into oblivion.

Fiscal Rocks and Political Hard Places

That same night, May 21, 2009, the city manager, the mayor pro tempore, and I all rushed back to Hermosa Beach for our preliminary budget meeting to discuss the city's finances for the coming year.

One of the main issues on our agenda that night had to do with staffing our fire department. The firefighters' union opposed a proposal by their own fire chief to maintain six firefighters on every shift but to leave the sixth position open during shifts when no firefighter was available. Five firefighters per shift could handle the vast majority of our calls. The fire chief told us that leaving the sixth position open would have no impact on the public safety. We had mutual assistance agreements with neighboring cities, so any truly large-scale emergency would be covered. We had been doing this for years and had never run into problems.

The firefighters' union opposed this proposal because when the sixth position came open, someone had to fill it, and that meant significant overtime for whomever that particular someone turned out to be. The fire chief estimated the overtime alone for filling the sixth position every time it was vacant would cost the city approximately $330,000 annually.

The vice president of the firefighters' union was one of the first people to speak at the budget meeting that night (more about him in another chapter). He told the city council that any cuts to fire department staffing were *dangerous for you people, and dangerous for us.*

The sixth man provided a safety margin the community could not reasonably do without, he said.

Singing Dieter Dammier's hymns, the union vice president talked about the largest dollar-loss fire in the history of Hermosa Beach, which occurred twenty years earlier. *Having that sixth firefighter would have prevented much of the damage,* he said.

The union front man also told us about a situation in which a man nearly died when his concrete sawing tool hit him in the neck. *There were only five firefighters on duty that day, and we nearly lost the man because of the department's understaffing,* he claimed.

Secret No. 8 – Have a Motor

He didn't explain how or why the sixth man would have made a difference. But that detail was beside the point. The important thing was that the city council was putting residents in danger, and the next person might not be so lucky.

Following the union vice president, two local moms took the microphone. The first, who identified herself as *a citizen and mother with a school-age child*, told us the city's budget should never be balanced at the expense of public safety. She fretted openly about her kids and what might happen to them if the firefighters did not get the sixth man guaranteed for each shift.

The second mom who spoke got right to the point. She presented a scenario in which a child on the baseball field was hit by a ball and somebody at the school fell off the playground at the same time. Because of the proposed *cuts* to the fire department, she said, one of our kids is potentially going to die.

The time that elapsed between Judge Meechum slapping the conference room table to a local mom telling me, on public access TV, that her kids were going to die was approximately six hours.

֍

The mediation was a failure, and a few days later we debriefed our colleagues about what had transpired with Judge Meechum. We used words like *sobering*, *crisis*, and *bleak* to describe our predicament. We reported that Judge Meechum believed Macpherson had a winnable case and had indeed suffered actual damages from the city's breach of contract. Although the evidence was not presented to us at the mediation, we understood from Judge Meechum that Macpherson could prove that the company had spent somewhere in the neighborhood of $8–10 million preparing to drill before the city pulled the plug on the project. This was much more than we expected, and it was not welcome news, because it set the baseline for restitution alone at a number approaching the outer limits of our ability to pay. We weren't even at the question of lost profits and damages yet.

We learned that Macpherson believed there were 30 to 40 million barrels of oil sitting just off our coast, and were it not for the breach of contract, the oil company would be exploiting those resources. It was no help that the price of oil at the time was approximately $100 per barrel. Our own expert was going to say there was only a maximum of 10 million barrels out there, and the oil was low quality and full of sulfur. Even so, if a jury used our best-case estimates about quantity and price to calculate Macpherson's lost profits, a settlement was still many millions of dollars more than we could afford.

Another aspect of the case—one we tended to discount because the financial part was so overwhelming—had to do with what Macpherson believed was right. There was a sense of outrage among the city council and residents that a faceless oil company would come to our little city and demand what amounted to a multimillion-dollar ransom because we were legitimately afraid of pollution in our city and on our beach. At the mediation, we learned for the first time there were human feelings on the other side too, and Macpherson's deep sense of injustice about what had transpired was no less intense than our feelings. He remembered very clearly what had transpired at the city council meeting all those years ago.

The wolf was at our door. Boyd Goodfellow and I reported all this to our colleagues. Kozlowski and Daley listened to the

Secret No. 8 – Have a Motor

news and looked grim. The Man Who Shakes His Head did. Macpherson knew our position, and we knew his. He believed the city had enough to fund the settlement he wanted but that we were unwilling to make the cuts necessary to do it. We believed we had turned over every rock and offered the best package we could. We were at an impasse.

We also learned that the judge in our case was holding firm to the trial date, and that there were going to be no more continuances or delays. We knew this because we had asked for one when one of our experts became ill and unable to appear at trial on the date scheduled. Losing him was going to be a problem for us, but the judge was keeping our collective feet to the fire, as judges are wont to do because it increases the pressure on both parties to settle. Lots of soul-searching occurs while you're preparing for trial, and sometimes settlements miraculously materialize when everyone is forced to peer over the edge into the legal abyss. There was going to be a trial here, and we were buckling in and bracing for impact.

※

The city council had steadfastly refused to extract our city from this litigation, and the cost of those decisions had compounded over time. The price for peace in 2009 was more than we could afford.

Whatever the cost of a settlement, we were ultimately going to pay in the future, and that did not include the millions in legal fees we had already burned through. In fiscal year 2008–09 we budgeted half a million dollars to defend ourselves in the Macpherson lawsuit. We budgeted $750,000 each year from

2009 through 2011, and in fiscal year 2011–12 we increased that amount to $1.1 million—roughly the same amount we planned to spend on citywide street improvements that year.

On top of this enormous cost, we also risked losing our ability to control our city's future. Daley's approach to this problem might have been politically astute in the short term, but over the long term it was a losing proposition. The council majority calculated that the political costs were greater than the risk of actually losing.

Litigation is an expensive and flawed approach to making policy decisions. It also rarely solves the actual problem, and often only makes it worse.

Or as a wise old lawyer once told me, *If you can resolve a case any way other than by a trial on the merits, do.* This is a rule all litigators live by, and city councils should too.

SECRET No. 9
Know Some People Won't Like You

Have a Good Story to Tell

The main problem Hermosa Beach faced as we marched toward trial with Macpherson was that we didn't have a clear, consistent story to tell the jury. The explanation for the city's decision to renege on its contract with the oil company was complicated, and much of the city's fitful decision-making over the years was impossible to explain.

(Of course, baked into the city's position was a newfound faith that oil, in all its forms and uses, was evil.)

The complexity, inconsistency, and moralizing woven into the fabric of the city's story made it too long to tell. The oil company, on the other hand, could put its theory of the case on a bumper sticker. As we would soon learn, the idea that people (and cities) were bound to do what they promised once they signed on the dotted line was something every juror understood.

Maybe the hardest part of becoming a politician is getting used to the idea that even when you win an election, half the people in your district may still not like you.

You may have sensible ideas, boatloads of charisma, and the endorsement of the pope, but someone, somewhere, will find a reason to oppose you. And those people can be vicious. But that's the deal. You got into this to change your community for the better, not to be universally liked. Avoid abandoning your ideals to avoid taking some heat. If heat is enough to scare you away, you may want to think hard before you decide to get into public office.

~

A mock trial is a dress rehearsal of the actual trial. Our lead trial attorney would put on the city's case and his second would put on the best approximation of what we believed would be Macpherson's. The mock trial was in effect, an intramural scrimmage.

The city hired a consulting firm to put together a statistically accurate jury pool that would analyze the results after the jurors had heard both sides of the case. The consultants asked the jurors which arguments they found persuasive and which evidence they thought the most important in forming their opinions. The consultants compiled these responses into a report that identified what worked and what didn't. Armed with this information, the lawyers could play to their strengths and buttress (or try to avoid) the weak spots in their case.

The information from the mock trial also helped us pick the jury. For example, we might learn that older married women were receptive to the city's health, welfare, and safety concerns. We might find that surfers and fishermen were hostile to the oil company's position, or that politically conservative jurors were skeptical of the city's motives. The aim, of course, was to try to select as many jurors as possible who fit a sympathetic profile for our case.

Statistically, the pool of mock jurors our trial consultants gathered were the same we could expect to see the first morning of trial. There were twenty-three men and twenty-seven women, ages twenty-one to sixty-seven. Fourteen were Hispanic, nineteen were white, ten were black, and seven were Asian. Twenty-four were married. Some had graduate degrees. Many had college diplomas. Two were widows. There was a retired FBI agent, a massage therapist, and a train conductor. It was truly a random sample of Los Angeles County.

These fifty mock jurors heard the trial team present both sides of the case. The results showed that we had real problems. For one, the jurors believed what most people do: a contract is a contract, and both sides are bound by what they agreed to when they signed it. The jurors thought it unfair that the city, having spent no money but standing to reap massive revenues, could unilaterally decide to breach the agreement and walk away scot-free.

We also learned that our *health, safety, and welfare* argument, the one Judge Meechum had told us was no better than a toss-up, wasn't even that. It didn't resonate with jurors at all. Many thought the report the city's consultant presented was nothing more than a pretext for canceling the project. Some jurors even went a step further and asked why the city allowed three years to pass between signing the contract and deciding to evaluate the potential health and safety impacts oil drilling might have on its residents.

We lacked good answers for any of these good questions.

Then there was the issue of Macpherson's lost profits. The city's lawyers argued that Hermosa Beach shouldn't pay millions of dollars for oil that Macpherson hadn't extracted and might not ever be able to get. Compounding the inaccessibility, our lawyers argued, was the fact that nobody was really sure if there was oil out there, anyway.

The jurors didn't buy it. One juror correctly summarized the biggest hole in the city's arguments: *Why would Hermosa Beach sign a contract with Macpherson in the first place if the city didn't think there was any oil in the Santa Monica Bay?*

He was right. There was no way to reconcile the city's willingness to sign a contract with the oil company in 1995 and its later claim that the jury should limit the oil company's damages because there wasn't any oil in the bay. The city's actions spoke louder than its words.

The most sobering and unexpected thing we learned from the mock trial was that many jurors wanted to *punish* the city for what it had done. Yes, punish. The jurors used that word.

This surprised us, because everyone on our side assumed the jurors would favor our quaint little beach city, with its surfers and volleyball players, over the rapacious oil company. We couldn't have been more wrong. The mock jurors saw Hermosa Beach as the Big G government, and perceived that we were backpedaling as fast as we could to avoid paying a just debt. As one juror said, *This* was *a situation of a bureaucracy trying to weasel its way out of a business deal.* The other jurors agreed.

And because the jurors thought the city had done wrong, they were willing to award Macpherson a sum with more commas and zeros than I could have imagined. The amount kept me up at night. The median amount the mock jurors awarded Macpherson after hearing both sides of the case was $284 million. Some jurors wanted to give the oil company as much as $551 million.

Hermosa Beach's total annual budget at this time was about $27 million.

The mock trial disabused us of our long-held assumptions about the case, and was therefore critically important to our decision-making going forward. Our position was weak, and the risks were larger than we had realized.

A Phone Call Changed Everything

I had not spoken to Don Macpherson since I saw him at the mediation with Judge Meechum in May 2009, so I was surprised when I got a phone call from him on the morning of Thursday, February 2, 2012.

The oilman didn't waste any time getting to his point. *I think there is a new opportunity for us to resolve the case without going to trial. Do you think the city would be interested?*

I had no idea what he meant, but the fact that he had taken the time to call me directly and not pass information through the skirmish lines of lawyers told me it was something significant. I was all ears.

Macpherson told me he had been approached by a third party, an oil company called E&B Natural Resources, that might be willing to help resolve the matter. E&B also had operations in California, and they had studied the reserves and were familiar with the litigation. E&B believed the political climate in town had changed, and they thought they could convince Hermosa Beach's residents to allow their project to go forward.

This was news to me, and I wondered what E&B knew about my city that I didn't. Perhaps they'd done polling that showed residents might now favor the project and revenues it would bring in? This seemed unlikely, but if these guys were willing to put up the eight-figure sum needed to settle the case, I figured they must know something.

Macpherson gave me the phone number for company's president—let's call him Herb McTweed. *Why don't you give him a call?* he said.

I asked Macpherson why he thought this strategy would work now, right on the eve of trial.

I want to sell my position, he said, *because I know the city can't compensate me.*

I couldn't believe what I was hearing. As excited as I was about the prospect of ending the litigation, I didn't want to seem too anxious to strike a deal. The trial would start in three months, and while I was listening to the oilman explain how we might resolve our differences, the lawyer in me was busily looking for the proverbial strings. Could this be true? Was it a trial tactic? Or a cruel ruse?

I thanked Macpherson for his call and agreed to contact Herb McTweed. As soon as we hung up, I called Boyd Goodfellow, who told me Macpherson had left him a message as well. We discussed the conversation I'd had with the oilman, and we agreed the new lead was worth pursuing. We decided it was best to keep whatever happened between the two of us, at least for now. There was nothing to get excited about yet, and if Gurney Frinks or The Man Who Shakes His Head or Cliff Clouseau got involved, we both knew the chances something going awry would increase exponentially.

Secret No. 9 – Know Some People Won't Like You

On Friday, February 3, I called McTweed at E&B Natural Resources. We introduced ourselves, spoke for just a few minutes, and agreed to meet for lunch the following Monday at a local restaurant. Goodfellow and I would come for the city and McTweed would bring his boss from E&B, a gentleman we'll call Antonio Fiore.

On Monday, February 6, we sat with McTweed and Fiore at a restaurant in El Segundo. The meeting was as uncomfortable as a blind date.

McTweed had the demeanor and gentle twang of a southerner, and the appearance of a federal prosecutor. Even in the Southern California sun he wore a dark Brooks Brothers suit and a conservative, striped, regimental tie. He had a regulation haircut and looked like a guy who probably liked baseball.

His boss, Fiore, was a man in his seventies who gave the impression that he was used to the finer things in life. With his slicked-back white hair, the New Yorker was one hearty *HOO-ah!* away from being an older version of Al Pacino's character in *Scent of a Woman*.

The only memorable thing about the lunch was that Fiore didn't say five words in a row from the time we sat down until the time we left. McTweed did all the talking. We never spoke about the political climate in the city or what we perceived our chances at trial to be. We made small talk about Hermosa Beach, our experiences in politics, and the weather. It wasn't long into the meeting that Goodfellow and I realized the two of them were clocking us, looking to see if we were people with whom they could do business. We were doing exactly the same thing.

A week later, on Monday, February 13, I got a call from Fiore. He thought there was a deal to be done and wanted to know our no-kidding number for settlement. I told him we were realistically able to get to about $10 million, but even that was going to hurt. Fiore said Macpherson was set on $40 million to walk away, and if we could come up with half of that amount E&B would put up the rest. This was disheartening, because there was no way the city could scrape together $20 million in cash.

I also gathered that Macpherson was putting this deal together on his own, maybe even against his lawyers' recommendations. *Don's lawyers are very bullish on the trial,* Fiore told me. I believed him. If the oil company's attorneys were doing the same things to prepare for trial that we were, I had no doubt they were bullish.

Soon after the phone call with Fiore, Boyd Goodfellow and I decided the discussions had reached the point at which we needed to involve our city attorney. The city attorney had been involved in the case for the past eighteen years, and had been there when this annoying litigation Godzilla that now threatened to eat our city had hatched.

The city attorney recommended that Goodfellow and I inform Gurney Frinks and the other three council members about the discussions we'd had with Macpherson and E&B. We did. Our colleagues didn't ask too many questions, but then again Frinks and Clouseau were freshly arrived in the city's litigation trenches and probably didn't even know where to begin. TMWSHH shook his head.

Boyd and I persuaded our three colleagues to appoint the two of us to be the city council's envoys, and we agreed to relay all developments to them. Like keeping bickering mothers away from the wedding planning, having these three at an arm's length from the day-to-day mechanics of the settlement talks was imperative to their success.

∽

Politics is an ask-heavy business. You ask for money and support to get elected. Once you're in office, you ask for support to get ordinances passed, policies changed, and decisions implemented. The asking is perpetual, and essential. The simple act of asking for so much and so often gives you insight into the weight of those asks.

It's one thing to ask someone to accompany you to a Lakers game, but it's very much another thing to ask someone to host a coffee sit-down in their home, particularly after you've made an unpopular decision or advocated for a difficult position. It makes the asking harder, but it also makes it gratifying to understand that if you ask, people will answer.

You *do* still have to ask, though.

An example: Years ago I attended a dinner with a number of local politicians. The dinner itself had gone well, marked by the sort of low-level conviviality that develops between colleagues after a glass and a half of cheapish Riesling.

Then the dessert came out.

It was borderline poisonous. Or maybe it was an experimental dessert nouveau. Hard to tell. Regardless, everyone at my table took a polite bite and then pushed their plates away.

That is, everyone but one veteran politician whom I knew from early in my city council career. He never received the sour-gooey monstrosity. Instead, a waiter brought him a tall glass of cold milk and a plate of freshly baked chocolate chip cookies. We sat around the table, passively listening to the presentation at the front of the room, while he dipped his cookies in milk and munched. Finally, I could stand it no longer. I leaned over and quietly asked, *Hey man, how'd you get the cookies?*

He smiled and leaned toward me. *I asked*, he said.

༄

Money, specifically who would end up paying what to whom, became the focus of the tripartite discussions between E&B, Macpherson, and the city. Money was what had brought E&B to Hermosa Beach in the first place, it was what had kept the parties from settling, and it was ultimately the only thing that would end the dispute. Over the next three weeks we engaged in intensive talks to work out a deal.

Macpherson eventually agreed to take a lump-sum $30 million cash payment in addition to a slice of the city's royalties if drilling occurred; this slice varied, ranging from 11 percent to 18 percent, depending on the location of the oil. I did not know what the city's royalties were in terms of dollars; I didn't care. Trading the present value of what was at risk for the future value of royalties we might never get was an absolute no-brainer.

The rest of the settlement agreement was structured like this: E&B would pay Macpherson $30 million and Macpherson would agree to drop its case against Hermosa Beach. In exchange for the payment and dismissal, the city would put the oil question before the city's voters. If Hermosa's residents voted the idea down, the city would repay E&B $17.5 million over a *commercially feasible time*, meaning whatever we negotiated with E&B.

The settlement meant the nightmare was over, and for the first time in more than two decades Hermosa Beach wouldn't have to deal with oil litigation. The looming threat of bankruptcy was gone. Instead of the hundreds of millions the mock jurors had told us we would pay, we capped our potential liability at $17.5 million and could stop shoveling hundreds of thousands of dollars a month into the litigation furnace.

Most important, the oil question would be decided by the residents of Hermosa Beach. Judges and juries wouldn't decide our future.

⁓

You meet a lot of people on the campaign trail. You listen to their concerns, you promise to faithfully represent their interests, and you build relationships. Keep those relationships. Be a familiar face.

People in sales will tell you that no one expects to make a sale the first time they meet someone, nor the second or third time. It takes repetition. People are generally more inclined to trust familiar faces.

Even if you haven't taken a lot of time to know someone, the constancy of a Christmas card or a regular e-newsletter can make you seem familiar enough for that voter to feel like they have a relationship with you. That's the first step toward motivating them to stand up when you ask for their support.

If you can repay their support by sincerely following through on your promises—or even just doing something small that you said you'd do—you'll go a long way toward reinforcing that familiarity with trust. Trust is what glues your supporters to you, but it must be maintained. Keep your positions steady, and know the weight of what you're asking.

The key to keeping supporters is to ensure that they always feel valued. I've always found that, regardless of the way you generally keep in contact, there is no substitute for a short, handwritten note when the situation warrants it.

※

On Friday, March 2, 2012, I stood in a conference room at our city attorney's offices with the E&B attorneys, McTweed, Macpherson, and his attorneys. Our legal team was there as was the city's current mayor, Gurney Frinks.

The meeting played out like a scene from a James Bond movie: E&B called their bank and Macpherson called his, the two sides exchanged top-secret codes, and in a flash of electrons $30 million changed hands. The principals signed the settlement documents, with the flock of lawyers for both sides hovering overhead like seagulls at a beach picnic. The sense of accomplishment and relief was palpable before the ink was even dry. There were smiles and backslaps all around. Lawyers who had days before been preparing to do battle shook hands and laughed with each other.

We did it! everyone thought. One side thought, *We won't have to declare bankruptcy!* And another side thought, *We just got*

Secret No. 9 – Know Some People Won't Like You

paid $30 million dollars! And the third side thought, *We have a chance to make a billion dollars!*

By design and necessity, Gurney Frinks had been kept on the fringe of the settlement discussions, but as the sitting mayor he was the person statutorily empowered to sign the settlement documents on the city's behalf. Earlier in the week he'd proudly instituted a smoking ban in all the public spaces of Hermosa Beach, and he was still emanating a self-congratulatory glow from this illiberal accomplishment. He had further impressed himself by getting his photograph on the front page of one of the weekly newspapers.

As soon as he signed the settlement agreement, Gurney Frinks stood up and told everyone within earshot that this was a banner week for him. This was a moment that most politicians would count as the highlight of their public service. How many people get to sign the document that eliminates an existential threat to their city?

As it turned out, the source of Gurney Frinks' excitement was a bit more basic than that: *I'm going to have my picture on the front page of the paper twice in one week!* he gushed. That quote contains everything you need to know about Gurney Frinks.

⁓

The following Monday, the city issued a press release announcing the settlement. The initial reaction to the news was surprise, followed by an outpouring of relief.

As the case inched closer to trial, I had started to field questions from realtors about the city's prospects. They asked things like, *If Hermosa Beach goes bankrupt, what will this mean for home values? Will the city be able to maintain services?*

These calls had become more and more frequent, which told me people were genuinely concerned about what was going to happen. People who might otherwise buy a home in town were probably thinking they would be better off in Manhattan Beach, or Redondo Beach, or someplace else nearby that didn't have a black cloud of bankruptcy hanging overhead.

I always told the realtors the same thing: *Don't worry, we're doing everything we can to prevent that from happening.*

But the truth was that it might have happened, and nobody really knew what would have happened to home prices, city services, or the quality of life in Hermosa Beach if we had gone to trial and lost. It was truly anyone's guess.

People stopped and thanked me in the supermarket and on the Strand. I got a handwritten note from a young lady in town who thanked me for saving the city, a note I kept in my desk to remind me of the good things we could do on the city council. Finding solutions to problems like this was the reason I'd entered the public realm in the first place.

Unfortunately, the goodwill didn't last for long. The honeymoon was less than two weeks.

Black or Green?

There's an old saying about politics: *Half your job is doing your job, and the other half is telling people what you've done.*

You can't just *do*. I know it feels like blowing your own horn to boast of your accomplishments, but your voters are unaware of what your job actually looks like. They lack the bird's-eye view of the situation that you have. In every case, be it budgeting, hiring, or choosing where to place a stoplight, your public has a fraction of the information you have. They need you to explain your actions in a way that they can easily understand. You need to explain yourself in a way that speaks to the people who need to hear you the most.

I wish that Boyd Goodfellow and I had gone on a traveling roadshow through our district to educate our constituency about what had happened with the settlement and what still needed to be done. It could have been as simple as a PowerPoint presentation outlining the history, the problems, and each of the flawed options, and then finally arriving at what needed to be done to move forward. We could have taken it to the PTA, the school board, the women's club, the Rotarians, and the historical society, each time tailoring the presentation to fit the audience.

Even if you have bad news to deliver to the public, you have to tell it in a proactive way. If you let the other side release the story to the public first, the chances increase that it will grow legs and run away from you.

Unchecked, a story can stir a population up into a political movement, and at that point there is no stopping it. You can position yourself as one of the speakers for that movement (and that can be useful for getting elected), but it's not a thing that you turn off like a tap.

Movements tend to be the result of the electorate's frustration finally bubbling to the surface. We saw this with Donald Trump's election: Trump clearly wasn't the most polished candidate in the field (the Republican primary was loaded with smooth, experienced politicians), but he listened to the voters, tapped into a groundswell of frustration, and rode that movement all the way to the White House.

So how can you tell if your district has a movement brewing? Listening closely to your constituency is the simplest answer. If you start hearing the same sets of opinions from a bunch of unrelated sources, you might be seeing the first bubbles of a movement. If you start campaigning just because you want to serve, but you start hearing the same set of atypical questions from every door you knock on, you might take that as a pretty solid clue that an issue is sprouting. If you can see the warning signs and really listen to the voters, you might be able to ride a movement to success.

༄

On March 13, 2012, we had our first city council meeting following the announcement of the settlement with Macpherson and E&B. To my surprise, six different people came to voice their acute vexation and opposition to what we'd accomplished.

I cannot tell you the outrage I stand here with, one visibly incensed resident told us. *The city council is acting like this is a voter issue. It's not. It's a legal issue.*

What were you thinking? another outraged resident demanded. *I wanted to see this played out in court. I think a jury would have better served our needs at this point.*

That city council meeting was my first direct, adversarial exposure to the anti-oil activists in Hermosa Beach. These anti-oil activists had the unswerving conviction that they alone knew The Truth about oil (and the Big-E environment), and that their Truth must be embraced. They were missionaries of a secular faith. For the anti-oil activists, a person could no more partially accept The Truth about oil than they could partially accept the truth about gravity. In fact, they weren't activists; they were Anti-Oil Evangelicals.

The Anti-Oil Evangelicals, I came to learn, spoke to people whose opinion about oil differed from theirs with the same mixture of contempt, condescension, and sadness one would expect from missionaries sent to convert a tribe of cannibals. At best, the Anti-Oil Evangelicals viewed people who did not share their views as unfortunately misinformed. The misinformed were environmental Philistines still capable of salvation. But on the other hand, some of the people who used oil were actually evil, like the cannibal who enjoys the taste of a well-barbecued neighbor.

As the Anti-Oil Evangelicals gathered momentum and spread The Truth to the disparate corners of Hermosa Beach, their message became bolder and more aggressive. Colombian drug lord Pablo Escobar had offered the noncompliant a choice: *plata o polmo*, silver or lead. In Hermosa Beach, the choice for the unconverted oil users and drilling proponents became as simple as the drug lord's offer—embrace The Truth or get the sword. Everyone would have to choose. There were no exceptions.

Of course, every cult has a leader, and the Anti-Oil Evangelicals' Jim Jones was a man named Jeff Cohn, and he was almightily infuriated the city council wouldn't drink his Kool-Aid.

Does that name sound familiar? It should. His father, David, was our newly elected city treasurer. As I would find out over the ensuing eighteen months, the Apple iPad doesn't fall far from the tree.

At that first meeting following the settlement, Cohn the Younger addressed the city council and calmly told us he opposed oil drilling. As he spoke, he placed a placard with his newly launched anti-oil website on the edge of the podium facing the television camera. The website was a repository for each and every conspiracy theory circulating among the Anti-Oil Evangelicals. And there were already a handful out there, only days after the settlement became public.

Also circulating among the Anti-Oil Evangelicals was the idea that the city would have won at trial.

Neat in a scholarly sort of way, calm, and otherwise well put together, Cohn the Younger's outward appearance gave no indication of his monomania. He had an attractive young wife and two cute, grade-school-aged children. Friends who knew him said that he was a regular guy—someone you could drink a beer with. But this one thing was a big deal, like having an otherwise normal friend who happened to fly into a murderous rage whenever he saw a cat or smelled peppermint. The oil settlement drove the outwardly well-adjusted, pleasant Cohn the Younger absolutely mad, and as time went on it became clear he could barely contain his fury.

An example: In the fall of 2013, I bumped into Cohn the Younger and his wife at a fundraising event for our schools. This was a wine-tasting event, where Hermosa Beach residents opened their homes to local parents in a secluded part of town. I randomly bumped into Cohn the Younger in the foyer of one home.

Secret No. 9 – Know Some People Won't Like You

Hello, I said, and commented on how lovely his wife looked that evening. I made a point to say hello to him whenever I saw him, because it's always harder to be angry with someone who is nice to you. I was doing my best to be as civil and pleasant as I could, and I certainly wasn't looking for a confrontation. So much for that.

As I stood in front of Cohn the Younger I saw the anger well up in his face. His wife must have seen it too, because she immediately started saying, *We're all here to enjoy ourselves. We're all here to enjoy ourselves*, like a soothing mantra. She must have seen this before, like a native who knows when the volcano is going to blow.

His wife tugging at his arm, Cohn the Younger nevertheless stood his ground, fists balled, and stammered through a lecture about how much he disagreed with *my* settlement. I listened, smiled, and told him I understood his concerns. But mostly I was hoping to escape the awkward moment without a physical confrontation. There were a few moments when I wasn't sure I would.

All the while Cohn the Younger's pleasant and now slightly embarrassed wife pulled his arm in the opposite direction. *We're all here to enjoy ourselves*, she kept saying, more and more loudly each time. Perhaps trying to convince herself of that too.

As time passed, the Anti-Oil Evangelicals became a fixture at the city council meetings and took their three minutes during the public commentary portion of our meetings to berate us and warn their fellow residents about the calamity that would befall our fair city if they voted for an oil project.

Cohn the Younger might have been the Jim Jones of the anti-oil movement, but they also had their own John Brown. Students of the Civil War may remember John Brown as the fire-and-brimstone antislavery crusader with wild eyes, a flowing white beard, and the ferocious conviction of an Old Testament prophet. Known for his brutal raids from the free state of Kansas into the Missouri territory, John Brown is widely recognized as being responsible for supplying the spark that eventually led to the conflagration that was the American Civil War. Although the Hermosa John Brown's beard wasn't quite as dramatic as the real John Brown's, ours was an eloquent speaker who preached about a coming civil war over oil in Hermosa Beach.

At the city council meeting on July 31, 2013, he said, *Forcing an election on this will create a kind of civil war. Everyone will have to pick a side: black or green.* Replace *black or green* with *slave or free*, and it could have been a speech from the Kansas Territory in 1859.

Hermosa John Brown laid out how the Anti-Oil Evangelicals would deal with the heretics, and how they would carry the fight to businesses (*many businesses would be identified as either for or against oil*) and into the schools (*What does little Suzy do when she learns that Billy's mommy and daddy support drilling that is ruining her neighborhood?*). Hermosa John Brown and the Anti-Oil Evangelicals also claimed to be afraid that *Hermosa Beach will be torn apart by the unfair election you're forcing upon us, feeding us into the jaws of Big Oil.*

Secret No. 9 – Know Some People Won't Like You

It was apparently lost on the anti-drilling zealot that he and his enraged congregation of Anti-Oil Evangelicals were the ones rending our town in two. Nobody from the oil company or anyone who supported the possibility of oil drilling threatened their neighbor's businesses. Nobody who was willing to consider the potential windfall to the city had singled out anyone else's children in school for ridicule or harassment. These were things that only Anti-Oil Evangelicals were talking about doing.

How good will our city be, Hermosa John Brown asked at one public meeting, without even a glimmer of irony, *if neighbor hates neighbor?*

About a week after the first city council meeting, Goodfellow and I had dinner at a restaurant in El Segundo with McTweed and some of the people who worked with E&B. McTweed wanted to introduce his team to us. Having just accepted $30 million of his company's money, we thought it would be impolite to refuse.

I naively thought my role concerning the oil issue was complete. Goodfellow and I had managed to extricate the city from the litigation, and whatever happened next was between E&B and the voters. I would make sure the city honored its obligations, but I had no intention of taking a partisan position. As I would later tell reporters, I was truly agnostic about oil. Of course, this was blasphemous to the Anti-Oil Evangelicals. Agnosticism was not an option. The Truth does not countenance ambivalence.

Nine Secrets for Getting Elected

In retrospect, the dinner was emblematic of how E&B and McTweed handled their business and the problems that lay ahead for them. They were only about halfway around the track on their victory lap, and they were still waving to the crowd. The people assembled at the table that night were getting their bearings, and they talked a lot about what they were going to do in *the future*.

At our meeting on March 13, Goodfellow and I got the first glimpse of the storm that was gathering, and we tried to relay to McTweed that the game was already afoot. We both told McTweed this was a political campaign, plain and simple. It was about convincing Hermosa Beach voters of the validity of their position; it was not about science or the mechanics of oil drilling. It might not even be about money, we said. The Anti-Oil Evangelicals were spreading The Truth, and as soon as they got organized they were going to be formidable.

McTweed, ever the proper Southern gentleman, listened and aw-shucks'ed and promised that E&B would do the same sort of grassroots outreach in the community where his opponents were. *E&B had resources,* he told us. *They would be aggressive. They were ready and experienced and well-equipped to handle the situation.*

E&B may have been an experienced oil firm, but they weren't ready or equipped for what hit them. Goodfellow and I could already see the looming fight would be a take-no-prisoners affair. We warned McTweed that outside environmental groups interested in stopping the drilling project would answer the call of an anti-oil *jihad* in Hermosa Beach.

Secret No. 9 – Know Some People Won't Like You

We learned later that E&B planned to approach this battle in their time-tested traditional way—through the firefighter's union. It had worked in other cities, and they thought it would work in Hermosa Beach too.

What's the connection between the firefighters and oil companies? Opponents of oil projects traditionally raise the alarm about the safety hazards drilling presents to the community. The oil companies' standard response to that charge was a promise to upgrade and expand the local fire department.

Of course the firefighters love this arrangement because it means more positions. More positions means more fire captains. More fire captains means more six-figure pensions at retirement.

It was a mutually beneficial relationship that worked because it was just obscure enough that most people couldn't see the connection, and the public generally trusted its firemen.

At the dinner that night, McTweed brought with him a high-ranking official from the Sacramento firefighter's union. He was a real somebody in the grand scheme of union politics, and that there was a position like his in the State Capitol relayed a sad message about California. He and I sat next to each other at dinner.

When the meal was over he took me aside. *You're not an asshole at all*, he said, a notable uptick in his voice. *Your local union guys said you were.* This realization seemed a genuine surprise to him.

Seemingly a decent enough guy himself, etiquette demanded I return the compliment. *Thanks*, I said, *You don't seem like an asshole either*.

Nine Secrets for Getting Elected

Because they traditionally focused on allying themselves with local fire departments, E&B's first and continued focus seemed to be on the Hermosa Beach Fire Department instead of the public, whose votes they would need. Meanwhile, the Anti-Oil Evangelicals continued to spread The Truth unopposed.

An acute lack of awareness about Hermosa Beach's political culture and a failure to understand their opposition left E&B woefully unprepared for what lay ahead. What might have succeeded elsewhere was not going to work here. They reminded me of the generals who learned that their cavalry was being decimated by a new invention called the Maxim gun in the opening battles of World War I. Waves of men on horseback, despite their glorious history and past victories, were no match for machine guns. Based on what I saw, E&B's generals' response to the machine guns would have been to order up more cavalry.

I also met with the Anti-Oil Evangelicals. Again, naively, I believed they were entitled to my time and attention just like anyone else, and that the best approach with them was detente. That assumption was incorrect. There were indeed only two choices for the Anti-Oil Evangelicals: *Black* or *Green*.

The emissary from the Anti-Oil Evangelical camp with whom I spoke most frequently was a youngish mother some might find attractive with a law degree. With her training in the law, she would come to city council meetings and make arguments that only someone with a law degree would make. She was determined, articulate, and tough.

Secret No. 9 – Know Some People Won't Like You

We met for coffee on a number of occasions to discuss the settlement, and each time we spoke I got the impression she understood my position. She would ask questions about different scenarios, and my response was always the same: The settlement was a godsend. *The people of Hermosa Beach will get to decide their own fate. Make your case to them,* I said. This is exactly how the democratic process is supposed to work. I wasn't going to take a partisan position.

She was always polite but never convinced. I didn't realize it at the time, but the pretty blonde mother sitting with me sipping her latte was offering me my last chance at anti-oil salvation. In her polite way, she was presenting me with the choice: *Black* or *Green*.

One time she made the point directly: *Why won't you just come out against oil?* I told her I thought it would be inappropriate for me to take a position for or against while the project wound its way through the city's administrative processes. Regardless of my personal biases about oil, I told her I needed at least to appear impartial on the dais.

If you did come out against oil, she said, *I could promise you a lot of votes.*

Turns out she was right. The Anti-Oil Evangelicals did muster a lot of votes on November 6, 2013.

They weren't for me.

❧

In January 2013, I was again mayor of Hermosa Beach, and for the next nine months I would be in the fight of my political life.

Nine Secrets for Getting Elected

By mid-2013, the Anti-Oil Evangelicals had become the preeminent political force in Hermosa Beach, and the folks willing to voice opposition had grown scarce. When the blood of the unbelievers runs in the streets, people tend to stay indoors.

The Anti-Oil Evangelicals gained political momentum, and as they did, their warriors became increasingly willing to use the sword against individuals or businesses that did not embrace their Truth. For example, a local wine shop with a small tasting room blasphemed by allowing E&B to host an event for its supporters. The wine shop was nothing more than a small business that was willing to accommodate paying customers. I knew the owners, and neither the shop nor its owners endorsed the oil project.

When the Anti-Oil Evangelicals learned the wine shop was abetting the infidels, they immediately began an e-mail campaign against the business. Remember, in Hermosa Beach in 2013 there were only two choices, *Black* or *Green*, and the Anti-Oil zealots had issued a fatwa against anyone profiting from the unbelievers. Faced with the public backlash generated by the Anti-Oil smear campaign, the wine company relented and declined to host the oil company's event.

The message that businesses and individuals who consorted with the infidels were just as guilty as the infidels themselves was not lost on the rest of Hermosa Beach.

On March 27, I was set to give the annual Chamber of Commerce State of the City speech, and I planned to use the forum as an opportunity to make the case for the settlement.

By this time, Cohn the Younger was hosting a website that floated a new conspiracy theory almost daily about the illegitimacy and illegality of the settlement. I disregarded the younger Cohn's incoherent ramblings, at least when it came to this. It was troubling however, that the settlement itself had begun to come under fire.

By the time I stood in front of a packed room of business owners, community leaders, and the public for my State of the City address, I was one of the few remaining Hermosans who dared to publicly challenge The Truth.

I did two things during my speech that evening that had not been done before. First, I shared with the public the mock trial you read about earlier. The public had never heard this information, and I thought it was important to show that the city council's decision to end the litigation short of trial had not been rash or cowardly, contrary to what the Anti-Oil Evangelicals were telling anyone who would listen.

I also told the audience about the bankruptcy case unfolding in Mammoth Lakes, California. This was new to the public. Like our city, Mammoth Lakes had signed a contract with a developer to build a hotel, but later changed its mind about the project. The developer sued and won a $30 million judgment. Mammoth Lakes litigated the case all the way to the California Supreme Court . . . and lost at every step along the way.

By the end of their litigate-to-the-death strategy, Mammoth Lakes had amassed a $43 million debt in interest and legal fees, including $2.3 million in fees paid only to the developers' attorneys, which the city was forced to pay; that $43 million did not include whatever Mammoth Lakes had paid its own lawyers.

When the litigation ended, Mammoth Lakes sought bankruptcy protection from the developer under Chapter 9 (the same chapter we would use if Hermosa Beach entered bankruptcy). This followed a last-chance offer from the developer for the city to pay $2 million up front, and then make annual installment payments of $2.7 million for the next thirty years. Mammoth Lakes, a town of 8,200 residents with a $19 million annual budget, refused.

What followed, I told the audience, were sharp budget cuts and recriminations. Mammoth Lakes sharply reduced services and staff, and the employees who remained took severe pay cuts. One of the developer's lawyers summarized Mammoth Lakes' approach to the litigation thusly: *They just keep putting their heads in the sand and hoping that some guy in a black robe will bail them out.*

Does any of this sound familiar? I asked.

⁓

I stood for reelection in November 2013, at the end of my second term as mayor. I finished fifth in a race in which the top three vote-getters won seats, and I trailed the fourth-place candidate, Cliff Clouseau, by two hundred votes.

I had been swept up and drowned in oil.

That election was a referendum on the settlement, and none of the three sitting city council members who had approved it held their seats. None of our replacements had ever held public office of any sort, nor served the city in any capacity before their election that November. They were committed Anti-Oil Evangelicals, and that was all that mattered.

Cliff Clouseau, despite his clear affirmations of The Truth and piety to Gods of No Drilling, still lost. The Anti-Oil Evangelicals held him accountable for his vote to settle the litigation and his willingness to make a pact with the oil company. Theirs is an angry god indeed.

On March 3, 2015, the voters of Hermosa Beach got the opportunity to do what the residents of Mammoth Lakes never did and vote on their own future. Hermosa Beach residents rejected the idea of oil drilling by almost a 4–1 margin. It was never close.

⁓

I lost my seat on the city council because I refused to pick a side during a movement. Periodically, there are movements in politics that overtake cities, states, and the country.

The year 2008 was a bad time to be a Republican, even a long-serving, well-respected one. President Obama's promise of "Hope and Change" swept the nation, and a few years later the Tea Party movement achieved political momentum, ousting long-serving politicians in both parties, and introduced Marco Rubio, Nikki Haley, and Ted Cruz to the national political stage. And in 2016 you were either on the Trump train, or on the tracks.

In 2013 the anti-oil movement seized Hermosa Beach, and it was a bad time to be an infidel—the Anti-Oil Evangelicals were going to make everyone choose a side, *Black* or *Green*.

Nine Secrets for Getting Elected

Running for local government is a hard, gritty process, one that in my experience is nastier than running for Congress. In local politics you're dealing directly with people who really, *really* care about the tree trimming in front of their houses, when the neighbor's trash cans get picked up, or how many parking spaces there are in front of their businesses. National politics normally feels more distant, more abstract.

Passions about local issues are fueled by a personal stake in whatever it is, sometimes fermented over years, dusted with resentment and the prospect of running into that particular so-and-so who is the source of the problem at the market. Local issues can have deep, personalized, and unseen roots, waiting for the right moment to erupt. Hopefully you'll see the eruptions coming.

Sometimes you won't.

CONCLUSION

June 6, 2006. I stood on the balcony of a supporter's home overlooking the Strand and the quiet nighttime beach. It was about 10:00 p.m. on Election Day. The absentee votes had already been counted and precincts were reporting their initial results.

I was going to win my first election.

When the evening began, I had only been accompanied by a few close friends and my staunchest supporters, but by this time of night the vote trends were obvious. People who could see the inevitable result were suddenly showing up at my party. The outcome was assured, and the pressure off. Laughter grew louder and the alcohol began to flow. The well-wishers multiplied and the congratulatory handshakes became frequent and more vigorous.

I stepped outside onto the balcony to get away from the growing crowd for a moment. A few minutes later, a longtime friend and former Hermosa Beach city council member wandered outside and joined me. The two of us leaned on the railing, looking across the deserted nighttime beach toward the dark Pacific.

Congratulations, Councilman Bobko, he said. He was the first person to address me with my new official title. I admit it felt great hearing that for the first time.

Conclusion

Then my friend slid a few inches closer to me, close enough that I could smell the flask in his hand contained Jameson's, not Bushmills.

He leaned in and passed me the little silver bottle. *Enjoy it,* he whispered, *because this is as good as it gets.*

∽

November 5, 2013. It was about 9:00 p.m. on Election Day. I was standing outside the restaurant on Pier Plaza where I'd held my election night party, looking for my younger brother. He'd just finished a shift in the ER at his hospital and was driving up from Orange County to join me.

The County Registrar had posted the absentee ballots online a few minutes earlier, and I was in fifth place. There were three seats available that election cycle, and the gap between my position and third place was two hundred votes. In a race in which the winner would need to collect a little more than two thousand votes, that gap was insurmountable.

I had already lost.

The result was particularly stinging because all the candidates who won were zealous Anti-Oil Evangelicals. The outcome was even more painful because the contest had been decided early that evening. A political bout everyone expected to go the distance turned out to be a first round TKO.

By 11:00 p.m. the issue was beyond doubt. I told the few people still at the restaurant that it was over, hugged and thanked them for sticking with me on a tough night, and my brother and I walked home.

After I called the other candidates and congratulated them

Conclusion

on their victories, my little brother and I sat in silence for a little bit. I eventually convinced him he needed to go home to his wife and baby daughter, and after he left I sat on my porch in the darkness and smoked the best cigar I had.

Alone.

∽

It would be easy to draw a straight line from June 6, 2006 to November 5, 2013, and determine success—or failure—if the ending point was higher than the start. But measuring success in public life isn't the same as measuring the success of your 401(k).

Maybe a better way to think of serving in public office is that it's like riding a roller coaster. There are soul-tickling highs followed by innard-rattling lows, made all the more exciting because sometimes you see them coming and sometimes you don't.

It will be exhilarating and scary, and at some point along the way, I can guarantee that people around you will be screaming.

The ride will also end. Sometimes suddenly. When it's over and you get off, you may tell yourself that you'll never do that again.

But before long, as you reflect on the experience and your heart rate returns to normal, you'll probably say the same thing about the roller coaster that you will about your time in public office—*Wow, that was fun!*

You're undertaking a challenging endeavor. Do your best. Stick to your values. Don't be afraid of failing.

Remember to enjoy yourself. The ride will be over before you know it.

HOW CAN WE HELP YOU WIN?

Now you know the nine secrets for getting elected!

I hope you've enjoyed learning about the process as much as I've enjoyed sharing it with you.

At this point, people often say, "I'm really excited and I love politics because I want to serve and make a difference, but I don't have time to do all that!"

We understand. The rest of your responsibilities—work, family, church, synagogue, or mosque—don't vanish into thin air just because you've decided to run for office. How do you find the time to accomplish everything you need to run a successful campaign while still devoting appropriate time to the other aspects of your life?

In order to help keep your life going *and* run a successful campaign, my team developed a suite of offerings ranging from a la carte campaign services to a complete, turnkey virtual campaign, which we will organize and run on your behalf. We can help you with services such as designing your campaign mail, identifying your target demographics, and of course—raising money.

We can provide all the behind the scenes support, encouragement, and guidance you need to make your election campaign easy, manageable, and fun.

How Can We Help You Win?

The beauty of the American system is voters decide who wins—no one can guarantee results. But we have the tools and know-how to increase your odds of success. Our experienced team can help get your campaign off on the right foot.

Visit www.electionsecrets.com to see the entire range of campaign services we offer.

You have a vision of how you want to serve your community, and you can see yourself accepting the congratulations of your friends and neighbors on election night after a victorious campaign.

Let us help you get there!